Lynn-Philip Hodgson

Inside-Camp X

"In War-time, truth is so precious that she should always be attended by a bodyguard of lies."

- Winston Churchill

Many of you have read about Camp X, the SOE, the OSS, the BSC, the FBI, the OWI and all of the other related secret organizations and how they intertwined. Their broad range of power affected the entire world, particularly during the years of the Second World War. You may not be familiar, however, with the inside workings of these operations and the manner in which they were created.

This is the inside story of Camp X!

Here you will learn about the hardships, the joys, the tragedies, the diligent work ethics and even the lighter side of life at Camp X. Imagine yourself inside Camp X, in the Officers' mess on a Saturday evening, drinking a beer or sipping a glass of wine and talking with some of the bravest, most talented military fighters alive at the time. Such was life Inside - Camp X.

During the 1970's, I was a Vice President of and the Director of Research for the Camp X Museum Society. Together with my wife, Marlene (Contributor), Alan Longfield (Editor), and Judi Longfield (Production Co-Ordinator), I served as the Associate Editor for the "Journal of the Camp X Society" which was transcribed and assembled from over forty hours of taped interviews which I conducted with many of the men and women who passed through Camp X during the war years.

It was with this and other related material that the true and authentic story of Camp X could be brought to light.

Inside-Camp X

Inside-Camp X

Lynn-Philip Hodgson

To: HAROLD

Hope you Enjoy it!

Copyright ©, Lynn-Philip Hodgson, 1999

Editor - Barbara Kerr

Blake Book Distribution
467 Fralicks Beach Road
Port Perry, Ontario
Canada L9L 1B6
(905) 985-6434
lhodgson@direct.com

Photo restoration and scanning by Jason Redwood
Cover design and page layout by Lindsay Burger

Printed in Canada

ISBN 0-88962-714-2 PB
ISBN 0-88962-721-5 HC

Second printing 1999.

To Mar, Ney and Kar and the Men and Women of Camp X

Table of Contents

Inside-Camp X

In Gratitude

I would like to take this time to thank the many people who were involved in so many different ways in making this book possible.

It is my firm belief that, because of these people, the 'Inside' story of Camp X will now live forever in the libraries of Canada and the story will be told over and over again in centuries to come.

The first person that I would like to thank is my editor, Barbara Kerr, who did a fantastic job of taking a very rough manuscript and turning it into the book it is today. I would also like to thank her for putting up with those cold, winter days in the den when we would fight over the house thermostat: me in my T-shirt and Barbara in her layers of sweaters and socks. Thank you, Barbara.

I would next like to thank my old friend, Alan Longfield. I have not only called upon my own memory, personal notes, interviews, and many hours of tape recorded interviews to put this book together, but I have also extracted from the published articles from '25-1-1' of which Alan was the Editor and I was the Associate Editor and Director of Research. Alan's masterful use of the English language and his creative talent helped me immensely in writing this book. These important stories needed to be told and thus be retained in the Canadian historical archives forever. I thank you again, Alan.

Alan's long hours and hard work were supplemented by those of his very talented wife, Judi, now a Canadian Member of Parliament. Many of our journal staff used aliases so that it did not seem that the journal was being put together by cutting and pasting at someone's kitchen table. Which, of course, is exactly how it was done. Judi Longfield's journal name was Judi Daigle. Her long hours of hard work resulted in the output of the Camp X Society's Journal, '25-1-1.'

Another contributor to the journal was Marlene Clark, Marlene Hodgson in real life and my wife of thirty five years. I would like to thank her for her contributions to the journal and subsequently to the production of this book. Marlene helped me in transcribing many hours of taped conversations and one can only begin to imagine what a tedious job that was.

I would also like to say thank you to the following people:

To Mrs. Otto, who was kind enough to give me a personalized tour of Camp 30, the German Officer's Prisoner of War camp at Bowmanville, Ontario, Canada.

To Mr. Charles Taws, the curator of the Bowmanville Museum, 37 Silver Street, who graciously allowed me to use pictures of Camp 30 which are a part of the museum's collection.

To Mr. Brian Winter, Archivist, 'Town of Whitby Archives', for information regarding and photographs of the Sinclair farm, "Glenrath".

To Mr. Bill Hardcastle, who, with his generous co-operation, made this book possible. Bill is highlighted throughout *Inside - Camp X* and contributed greatly to the authenticity of its contents.

To my old friend, the late Andy Durovecz, who wrote the introduction for my book. I hope you are in a better place, Andy, and finally free of pain.

To my good friends; Glen Copithorn for his research of Camp 30, Greg Wuerth for picking me up so often at the "Go" train and chauffeuring me around the Whitby and Oshawa areas, and of course, I could not forget Larry Grasby who helped me with the computer logistics.

To Jason Redwood, who appeared out of nowhere one day as I was looking at mounting expenses, not knowing where to go next with this project. Jason said, "I'll prepare it for typesetting on my Apple computer. I don't want a penny for it. It will give me a chance to learn my new computer." Jason, my friend, we will work something out, and many thanks again.

To Mac McDonald, who contributed greatly to this book. His stories of the Lighter Side of Camp X will remain with me forever.

To Susanna Rugly for the Hungarian translation.

To my new friend, Joe Gelleny. Thank you for your story.

And finally, to the Foreign & Commonwealth Office in London, England, for authenticating much of the content of this book.

Introduction

By Andrew Durovecz (a.k.a. Andy Daniels)

It gives me great pleasure to have been requested to write the introduction to a book which is intended to bring to light various and, until now, seldom mentioned but most dangerous aspects of the Second World War. The war was characterized by being the first war in history with a political ideological content.

The war was incubated in the ambitious twisted mind of the misfit, Adolf Hitler, who had a dream of establishing a great "National Socialist" (Nazi) Empire that would last for a thousand years. As a tragic irony, Hitler found an ardent supporter for his hellish fantasy in the person of the contemporary British Prime Minister, Neville Chamberlain.

As a fate of history, Winston Churchill reappeared on the political scene and, having departed from his earlier sharp right wing attitude and taken a more realistic outlook, put his "anti-Bolshevik" stand behind him, extending a friendly hand to Joseph Stalin of Russia. This brought about the "Anti-Fascist great alliance" involving all the anti-Nazi forces of the globe.

This effort is reflected in Churchill's timely remarks in which he declared;

" My message to you is one of greater hope than I have ever had in my life before. There is a spirit abroad in Europe which is finer and braver than anything that tired continent has known for centuries and which cannot be withstood... It is the confident will of whole peoples who have known the utmost humiliation and suffering and have triumphed over it, to build their own life once and for all. There is a marvelous opportunity before us and all that is required from Britain, America and Russia is imagination, help and sympathy. Four years of Nazi occupation has made the issue very clear... 1944 is going to be a good year, though a terrible one."

Learning the horrible lessons of World War II inspired the foresighted people of Europe to create a World Peace movement. This sensibility could be appraised as the greatest human endeavour of the Twentieth Century. At the threshold of a fast approaching new century, the world wide view of the human race is; "Peace."

As the book is so appropriately titled, *Inside-Camp X*, that too is where I was trained in 1942 "behind enemy lines" as a secret agent with the principle purpose of destroying Fascism. My greatest wish and high hope today is that the concerned leaders of all the nations will venture forth in an extensive program of producing for all human needs.

At the threshold of the new century, there could be nothing greater and more blessing on the human race than an avowment by all nations that "There shall be war no more!"

(Author's note: Andy passed away only two months after writing this introduction. Other than Christmas cards back and forth, I had not communicated with Andy for several years as he did not have a phone. It was truly ironic and must have been fate that one day, before I had even begun writing, I awoke and said to myself, "I have to write a letter to Andy today asking him to write an introduction to my book."

The world lost a great man in Andy Durovecz. His mission did not single-handedly change the course of the war but, together with the hundreds of other secret agents acting as a united team, they not only caused Adolf Hitler to assemble an entire department of counter-intelligence agents, but also undermined the war progress that the Germans were making, vis-a-vis the agents' successes in sabotage.)

*2. Andy Durovecz (left) and Marlene Hodgson (centre)
at the Camp X Reunion, April, 1979*

Introduction

By Lynn-Philip Hodgson

WHAT WAS CAMP X?

Unofficially known as Camp X, the paramilitary training installation was officially known by various names: as S25-1-1 by the RCMP (the Royal Canadian Mounted Police file name), as Project-J by the Canadian military, and as STS-103 (Special Training School 103) by the SOE (Special Operations Executive), a branch of the British MI-6. It was established December 6, 1941, at Whitby, Ontario, Canada through co-operative efforts of the British Security Co-Ordination (BSC) and the Government of Canada.

The BSC's chief, Sir William Stephenson, was a Canadian from Winnipeg, Manitoba, and a close confidant of the British Prime Minister, Sir Winston Churchill, who had instructed him to create "the clenched fist that would provide the knockout blow" to the Axis powers. One of Stephenson's successes was Camp X!

The book, *Inside-Camp X,* and the story begin, "Lieutenant-Colonel Roper-Caldbeck, the first Commanding Officer of Camp X, stopped, stared over the rolling fields, picturesque Lake Ontario, and the newly erected buildings and thought to himself, *"Everything is ready!"*

The Date: December 6th, 1941!...

That date was most significant. Had the Japanese attack on Pearl Harbour been executed six months earlier, there would never have been a Camp X. The

Camp was designed for the sole purpose of linking Britain and the United States. Until the direct attack on Pearl Harbour, the United States was forbidden by an act of Congress to get involved with the war. How timely that Camp X should open the day before the attack on Pearl Harbour by the Japanese.

Even the Camp's location was chosen with a great deal of thought: a remote site on the shores of Lake Ontario, yet only thirty miles straight across the lake from the United States. It was ideal for bouncing radio signals from Europe, South America, and, of course, between London and the BSC headquarters in New York.

The choice of site also placed the Camp only five miles from DIL (Defense Industries Ltd.), currently the town of Ajax. At that time, DIL was the largest armaments manufacturing facility in North America.

Other points of strategic significance in the Camp's locale include the situation of the German Prisoner of War Camp in Bowmanville, the position of the mainline Canadian Pacific Railway which went through the top part of Camp X, and that of General Motors on the eastern border of the Camp. The Oshawa Airport which was a Royal Canadian Air Force (RCAF) / Royal Air Force (RAF) Commonwealth air training school at the time was only a short drive from Camp X. Each of these points will be delved into in more detail throughout the book.

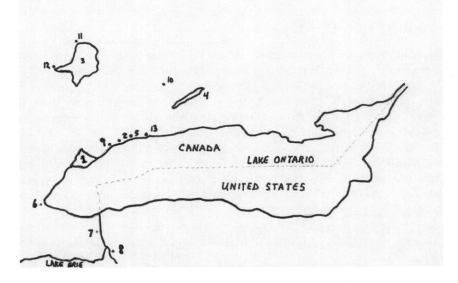

3. Map of Lake Ontario and the borders of Canada and the United States

Points of interest; (all distances are approximate and relative to Camp X)

1 - Toronto, Ontario, Canada - twenty five miles from Camp X and sixty five miles from the US via road

2 - Whitby, Ontario and the site of Camp X

3 - Lake Simcoe, Ontario - Canadian military basic training at Camp Borden - fifty miles

4 - Rice Lake, Ontario - the site of the secret agents' training. (This is where the agents would be dropped off and left to find their way back to the Camp as described in Chapter III) - thirty miles

5 - Oshawa, Ontario - the site of The Oshawa Airport about five miles away, and General Motors, adjacent to Camp X

6 - Hamilton, Ontario -sixty miles

7 - Niagara Falls, Ontario - eighty miles

8 - Buffalo, New York, USA - ninety miles

9 - Ajax, Ontario - five miles

10 - Peterborough, Ontario - forty miles

11 - Orillia, Ontario - fifty five miles

12 - Barrie, Ontario - fifty miles

13 - Bowmanville, Ontario - site of Camp 30, the German POW camp - twenty miles

The Commanders of the Camp soon realized the impact of Camp X. Requests for more agents and different training programs were coming in daily from London and New York. Not only were they faced with training agents who were going to go behind enemy lines on specialized missions, but now they had been requested to train agents' instructors as well. These would be recruited primarily from the United States for the OSS (Office of Strategic Services) and for the FBI (Federal Bureau of Investigation). Soon there were trainers training trainers for new Camps that would be set up in the U.S., primarily at RTU-11 in

Maryland.

To ease the demand for trained trainers, Lieutenant Colonel R. M. Brooker, a British SIS (Secret Intelligence Service) man, established a particularly successful program of weekend courses for OSS executives. (When Camp X opened, the OSS was officially known as the Co-Ordinator of Information (COI) and did not become the OSS until June of 1942).

The psychological aspect of the training was most critical. As crucial as the agent's training in silent killing and unarmed combat was the development of his ability to quickly and accurately assess the suitability of a potential "Partisan." He had to be able to recognize a would-be recruit by being alert at all times and in any situation. He was trained to listen for a comment about the government, about the Nazis or about how the war was progressing, and to subsequently engage the individual in conversation, perhaps offer him a drink or buy him a meal. In this manner he could further identify the individual's philosophy and thoughts about the war.

Paramount among the objectives set for the operation, including the training of Allied agents for the entire catalogue of espionage activities (sabotage, subversion, deception, intelligence, and other 'special means'), was the necessity to establish a major communications link between North and South America and European operations of SOE. Code named 'Hydra', the resulting short-wave radio and telecommunications centre was the most powerful of its type. Largely "hand-made" by a few gifted Canadian radio amateurs, Hydra played a magnificent role in the tactical and strategic Allied radio networks.

When one steps back and looks at the 1940 grand picture, one can see exactly why Canada was so important to the SOE as a base for their agents: if the agents were to be recruited in Canada, why not train them there? Soon the BSC had large populations of French Canadians, Yugoslavs, Italians, Hungarians, Romanians, Chinese and Japanese at their disposal and in a concentrated geographical area. It was easier to send a few instructors over to Canada then it was to send 500 or 600 potential agents to Britain only to find that they were not Secret Agent material and afterward have to send them home. One must remember that the British were still an invasion target to the Germans. Such an invasion, if successful, would be the end of the SOE Training Schools in Britain. Thus, Camp X became the assembly line for 'special agents' and subsequently the SOE.

The agents trained at Camp X would have no idea whatsoever as to their future mission behind enemy lines, nor for that matter would the instructors and/or the Camp Commandant. Camp X's sole purpose was to develop and train all agents in every aspect of silent killing, sabotage, Partisan work, recruitment methods for the resistance movement, demolition, map reading, weaponry, and Morse Code.

It was not until the agents completed their ten week course that the instructors and commanding officers would assess each individual for his particular expertise and subsequently advise the SOE in London of their recommendations. For example, one agent might excel in the demolition field while another might be better at wireless telegraph work.

Once the agents arrived in Britain, they would be reassessed and would be assigned to a Finishing School where their expertise would be further refined. Once this task was completed, another branch of the SOE would take over and develop a mission best suited for each individual agent.

Eric Curwain, Chief Recruitment Officer of the Canadian Division of the British Security Co-ordination, wrote about Canada's significant contribution to the war effort in his unpublished manuscript, *Almost Top Secret*.

"Previous visits to Canada could not prepare a wartime visitor for the vast war effort that at once became visible on leaving the port of Halifax to take the train for Toronto. Any Allied national from Europe must have been thrilled to see those long lines of loaded freight cars, lying in sidings, awaiting the day to pour their weaponry into the hundreds of ships that Germany's ever-increasing hordes of submarines could never defeat."

As part of my research into Camp X, I have been in constant contact with London, England, and specifically the FCO (Foreign and Commonwealth Office). One interesting piece of information from London I would like to share with you now. The following is an excerpt from a letter which I recently received from Duncan Stuart, SOE adviser, FCO.

"First of all, I should say that virtually no records have survived over here about STS-103. As I am sure you know, there was a bonfire of all of the New York and Canadian records at STS-103 at the end of the War. And, in any case, Bill STEPHENSON (sic) was not much in the habit of informing SOE HQ of the details of what he was up to, so there was never much information on American or Canadian matters in HQ. Moreover, SOE's Training Section over here destroyed all its training records at the end of the War."

Thus, it will be books such as *Inside-Camp X* that we will have to rely upon to tell the real story of what went on behind those barbed wire fences. To meet this end, I have accumulated forty hours of taped interviews with the men and women of Camp X as well as the neighbors of the Camp. I personally spent hundreds of hours investigating and researching in order to produce *Inside-Camp X*.

4. The author, Lynn-Philip Hodgson, at Camp X, November, 1977

Chapter I

The Start Up

Lieutenant-Colonel A.T. Roper-Caldbeck, immaculately dressed in his British Officer's uniform, opened the front door of the old farm house and stepped out into the cold winter's day. It had snowed the previous night. The brilliant sunlight reflected off the snow and the deep blue lake.

As he looked around, he could see the newly erected asbestos shingled huts, the sloping farm land and the beauty of Lake Ontario. He walked down the steps and started along the narrow roads that connected the various buildings. The snow was crisp and crackling under his feet. He walked slowly past an ominous looking building, strange with its very highly placed windows. He knew, of course, that this was Hydra, the top secret radio transmitting building that would receive data from all around the world.

As he turned toward the south, he passed by the agents' barracks, empty now but soon to be filled with Special Operations Executive (SOE) agents-in-training. He knew all too well what was in store for the young men who would pass through Camp X. After their training in Canada, they would go on to Britain for further training before their personalized missions could take place. He fully understood that, of the agents who would be trained at Camp X, many would not return to their homes. As he turned another corner, he could see the Jeep off in the distance on its winding path traveling the circumference of the camp, constantly on guard.

Lieutenant-Colonel Roper-Caldbeck, the first Commanding Officer of Camp X, stopped, stared over the rolling fields, picturesque Lake Ontario, the newly erected buildings and thought to himself; *"everything is ready!"*

The Date: December 6th, 1941!...

5. Lieutenant-Colonel A.T. Roper-Caldbeck (center, in kilt) and his staff

Britain had her back to the wall. The Nazis were about to leap across the channel and strike at the throat of England.

Lieutenant-Colonel Roper-Caldbeck had a very serious task ahead of him as he knew that his mission could make the difference in the final results of this war, the war to end all wars!

Much has been written about the Second World War and of the various intelligence organizations. *Inside - Camp X* will primarily concentrate on the Secret Intelligence Service (SIS - British), Special Operations Executive (SOE - British), British Security Co-Ordination (BSC - British/North American), Federal Bureau of Investigation (FBI - United States), Office of Strategic Services (OSS - United States), Office of War Information (OWI - United States), and the Royal Canadian Mounted Police (RCMP - Canadian).

Early on in the war, Winston Churchill recognized the importance of a solid intelligence network and the role that it would play in the defeat of the Axis countries. It is with this knowledge that he would call upon the Secret Intelligence Service (SIS) and then upon a branch of the SIS, the Special Operations Executive (SOE).

With this in mind, and recognizing that the Nazi regime also had sights on North and South America, he created the British Security Co-Ordination which was charged with protecting the Americas. It was at this time that William Stephenson was introduced to the intelligence community and appointed Head of the British Security Co-Ordination (BSC). The

BSC and the SOE had a special liaison that worked well and quickly enabled them to link up with the United States Office of Strategic Services (OSS).

General (Sir) Colin Gubbins, the chief of the SOE, charged with the challenge to "set Europe ablaze", said after the war, "Per capita, the secret war was bloodier than the Somme. The only difference was that the cries were muffled and, in many instances, the corpses were never found."

* * *

The Introduction of the 'Start Up' Camp X Personnel;

The unofficial Commandant of Camp X was a Colonel Lindsay of the British Army. Colonel Lindsay was sent to Canada in September of 1941 to meet with Tommy Drew-Brook, head of the Canadian wing of the BSC (more on the BSC later), and others in order to lay the groundwork for the Camp. Lindsay was, to say the least, unimpressed with Canada. The weather was miserable while he was there and left him with a bad impression of the country. Upon his return to England, he wasted no time in informing his second in command, Major Brooker, "I won't be going back". Somehow, he successfully convinced Colin Gubbins, head of SOE, that he should not return.

* * *

6.

Lieutenant-Colonel Arthur Terence Roper-Caldbeck, born June 16, 1906 in Scotland, joined the regular army as a member of the A & S (Argyll and

4

Sutherland) Highlanders. On August 11, 1941, he joined the SOE and in December of the same year he was told that he would be going to Canada to head up a "Special School" and indeed was appointed the first official Commandant of Camp X.

Lieutenant-Colonel Roper-Caldbeck knew that his stay in Canada, specifically at Camp X, was going to be a good one by virtue of the gifted officers that were assigned to Camp X. They were, after all, some of the world's most talented men in their trade.

7.

Lieutenant-Colonel Richard Melville (Bill) Brooker was born in Paris, France, on September 23, 1909. He joined the SOE's training section on March 18, 1941, with the rank of Captain. In December of 1941, he was sent to Canada along with Lieutenant-Colonel Roper-Caldbeck, with the rank of Major as second in command of STS 103 (Special Training School # 103, Camp X).

With his promotion to Lieutenant-Colonel, Brooker would succeed Roper-Caldbeck as Commandant of Camp X when the latter would return to England in 1942.

After the war, Bickham Sweet-Escott wrote the following regarding the importance of Camp X and Lieutenant-Colonel Bill Brooker:

"I have no doubt that OSS (Office of Strategic Services) got much more out of our training school in Canada (Camp X), than from all the efforts of our party in Washington.

"What was unique about Oshawa was the personality of the commandant, Lieutenant-Colonel Brooker. Bill Brooker was a born salesman. He was a brilliant and convincing lecturer, and he had an immense wealth of stories from the real life of a secret agent to illustrate his points."

* * *

8.

Lieutenant-Colonel Cuthbert Skilbeck was the third and final Commandant of Special Training School - 103 (Camp X)

When the OSS put pressure on the BSC for Bill Brooker's services, it quickly became necessary to replace him. The logical successor was Major Cuthbert Skilbeck, the second in command. Skilbeck's background was very similar to many others who would come through the SOE, BSC and OSS. He had lived in Europe for some time before the war and spoke both German and French fluently. Men such as Skilbeck were naturals for this type of war work and were in great demand.

Like Roper-Caldbeck, Brooker and most of the other British Camp X officers, Skilbeck was yet another 'Beaulieu' alumni, which was the 'ACE' of the secret agents' finishing schools in Britain. Therefore, he was a natural choice to succeed Brooker when the time came. They had been trained together, had been instructors together and had become good friends.

After the war, the FCO (Foreign & Commonwealth Office) wrote the following about Lieutenant-Colonel Skilbeck in response to my inquiries:

"After serving as FSO (Foreign Service Officer) at Marseilles in June of 1940, he became an Instructor at the I. Corps Intelligence Training School at Matlock. While there, he was recruited by SOE to be an instructor at Beaulieu from April 1, 1941. In September 1941 he became Chief Instructor of the Group B (Finishing) Schools at Beaulieu with promotion to Major. He left for Canada via the USA on July 30, 1942 on posting as Chief Instructor to STS 103, of which he later became Commandant with promotion to Lieutenant-Colonel, in succession to Brooker in March of 1943. Following the closure of STS 103 he arrived back in the UK on April 28, 1944 and with effect from August 12, 1944 he was posted from SOE to the Political Intelligence Department of the FO (Foreign Office) for special duties."

9.

Lieutenant-Colonel William Ewart Fairbairn, General List, was born February 28, 1885, in Rickmansworth, Herts, England. Prior to the Second World War, Fairbairn was the Chief Instructor at the Shanghai Municipal Police from October 1907 to March 1940. Fairbairn joined the SOE in March 1942 with the rank of Captain, having previously been an instructor at the War Office Special Training Centre in Scotland in July of 1940. Immediately after joining the SOE, he was posted to STS 103 (Camp X) as Chief Instructor and granted local rank of Major on June 8, 1942. Lieutenant-Colonel Fairbairn was fifty seven years old when he accepted this assignment to physically train men thirty years his junior! Lieutenant-Colonel Fairbairn was unquestionably the most experienced and accomplished person at that time in the art of 'silent killing'. The fact that Fairbairn was sent immediately to *Camp X* attests to the importance that the British Secret Service put on STS 103.

* * *

10.

Major James (Paddy) Adams, born June 22, 1905, in Donagadee, Northern Ireland, was a member of the Royal Corps of Signals. He joined the SOE November 8, 1941, and left for Canada December 22, 1941. Major Adams was appointed Signals Instructor in Camp X and helped build the wireless station, 'Hydra'.

Paddy's primary function at Camp X was to train the agents in becoming as proficient as possible in the use of W/T (Wireless/Telegraph) radios and Morse Code. It is said that his accent was so thick that often the agents-in-training could not understand him which would infuriate Paddy to no end.

* * *

11.

Major Arthur Jackson Bushell was born in Toronto, Ontario, May 10, 1895. Prior to the war, Major Bushell was a merchant. He joined the Canadian army at the outbreak of hostilities and was recognized at an early stage as "fine officer material". On December 6, 1941, Major Bushell was assigned to Camp X as the Adjutant-Quartermaster and Lieutenant-Colonel Roper-Caldbeck's right hand man. A Canadian, Bushell's responsibility was to be the liaison between the Canadian NCO's and the British Officers to ensure that things operated smoothly at the Camp.

* * *

12.

Major Frederick Stanley Milner was born March 26, 1916, in Birmingham, England. At the outbreak of the war, he joined The Dorset Regiment. He was transferred to SOE in February, 1941, with the rank of Lieutenant. He sailed to Canada on November 21, 1941, and, upon arrival, was assigned to Camp X as 'Training Instructor', his field of expertise, demolition. Many SOE, FBI and BSC dignitaries would be treated to a fascinating exhibition of "fire works" by the ever-popular Major Milner.

* * *

13.

Sergeant-Major George de Rewelyskow was the final major player in this talented and colourful group. His specialty was 'small arms' and 'unarmed combat'. De Rewelyskow was one tough man. He was afraid of nothing and was certainly one of the best choices for this important assignment at Camp X.

On one particular Saturday night at the Camp, de Rewelyskow, of whom it was said, "could strike like a snake", went into Oshawa for some "R&R" with one of the other instructors. After some time at the Genosha Hotel, de Rewelyskow noticed that a man was staring at him and making gestures. De Rewelyskow quickly became agitated and went over to confront the man. Some words were exchanged and suddenly the man took a swing at de Rewelyskow. In one continuous motion, and with split second timing, de Rewelyskow grabbed a ketchup bottle, broke it and held the jagged edge to the man's throat until finally his mate pulled him away. This man never knew how lucky he was for he had just taken on one of the most feared silent killing experts in the world.

* * *

14. Mac McDonald on guard duty

(Mac) McDonald, known only as Mac as there were no last names at Camp X, was daydreaming in his Jeep one cold December day in 1941. "Where am I," he asked himself, "how did I get here, and what is this place?" In time he would find out, but for now his strange orders were to guard the Camp from unwanted visitors, shoot to kill, ask questions later! What could be going on here on the shores of lake Ontario, so far from the battles of World War II? Mac thought about how much things had changed since that morning when he had sat with his mates at the Horse Palace in the Canadian National Exhibition in Toronto, awaiting his assignment. Would he be going overseas and, if so, when?

Thinking back further, Mac remembered being pulled out of the line by his sergeant, Old Birmingham, who said, "Sorry Mac, you're not going with us. You are wanted in Toronto." The troops had left so quickly that they had taken Mac's papers with them. He went back to the Horse Palace where he reported to the Commanding Officer and told him what had happened. The CO did not know what to do with Mac and told him to await further instruction. Unfortunately, Mac could not be paid as Old Birmingham had ordered that the men not be paid until they had actually boarded the train.

As it took three weeks for his orders to come through, Mac was forced to take a leave of absence while he waited for his papers ordering him to be shipped to Hong Kong. Just as they were about to ship out, once again the Sergeant rushed up and said, "These two guys aren't going".

The two were told that they were needed for 'Special Duties' in Toronto. They were also told that they would be assigned to be guards at a special camp and they were ordered to sign the oath of secrecy under the 'Official Secrets Act'.

Mac and six others were loaded into the back of an open truck. As they drove along the King's Highway # 2, it began to snow making the forty five minute drive a long, cold trip.

The truck had been filled with rations, dishes, pots, pans and other miscellaneous items which they had been ordered to assemble. When they arrived, Sergeant Maloney was there to greet them. Except for a night watchman, Maloney was the only person at the Camp. The night watchman was promptly dismissed. Mac and the other newly-arrived guard took over from that moment on.

From this point in time the "Military Machine" began to pick up speed. Within half an hour of Mac's arrival at the Camp, four British corporals landed. Half an hour later, the Captain and the Sergeant-Major landed. Within another half hour, Adjutant-Quartermaster Bushell landed. And in another hour, the Commanding Officer Lieutenant-Colonel Roper-Caldbeck and the Second-in-Command Major Brooker arrived. It was only the third week of January, 1942, when the first OSS agents started arriving for their "Special Training".

Mac recalls that the Commanding Officer's residence was not completed until the end of January, 1942. In the interim, the CO stayed in the old Sinclair house. A small root cellar near the farmhouse doubled as a munitions magazine. Later on, as the need arose, additional magazines were built just north of the large barn.

A few months after the December 6, 1941 opening of Camp X, Bill Hardcastle was at his desk at The Toronto Star doing his normal daily routine. After work, Bill headed home as he would do any other night, but this night would be special. This night would completely change his life forever!

15. Bill Hardcastle was one man who took his job very seriously. On his breaks and when off shift, Bill could always be found reading books on Morse Code. When he was not reading about it, he was practicing on his portable 'Suitcase Radio' for the day that he might be called upon to head out to the "Field" on a mission to some far off country and the unknown.

As a matter of course during war time, a citizen can be called upon to serve his country at a moment's notice. When Bill Hardcastle was called to do so, he responded immediately.

Bill lived with his parents at their home in Toronto. He was sitting in the living room that fateful evening when the telephone rang. His mother answered it and said, "Bill it's for you." Bill picked up the phone and a man on the other end of the line identified himself as Bill Simpson (a.k.a. Eric Curwain).

16. Eric Curwain (a.k.a Bill Simpson)

He asked if Bill "would be interested in a job in communications." Bill replied "that he was interested indeed." Simpson said that he had heard that Bill was a very good "Ham" (Amateur Radio Operator), and that he could receive code (Morse Code) very quickly. Bill modestly muttered something about being "average", he supposed. Simpson then asked Bill if he would be interested in meeting with him, perhaps at "Simpson's Department Store or The Royal York Hotel." Bill suggested "Stoodleigh's Restaurant at the corner of Bay and Wellington."

"How will I know you?," Bill asked.

"Just give me your description. I'll be at the back of the restaurant. We'll have dinner together."

"The next day, Bill arrived at the restaurant as agreed. Simpson recognized Bill immediately, and they talked about how Bill felt about the job that had been outlined to him. Simpson asked Bill where he was working, and Bill told him that he was employed by The Toronto Star in the advertising department. Simpson said he would speak to Bill's boss, a Mr. Tait, the General Manager, to arrange for his departure. Simpson then suggested a salary which was most acceptable, and concluded by stating that Bill would be meeting another gentleman in a few days at the Royal York Hotel, also in Toronto."

17. Tommy Drew-Brook

Tommy Drew-Brook was seated at his usual table in the cafe of the Royal York "where a full suite served as his accommodation - a sure sign of his prestige." He looked down at his watch and noted that he had another ten minutes until his scheduled appointment was to arrive. He was hoping that this individual would be acceptable as time was of the essence. Camp X had opened December 6, 1941, and here it was, March of 1942, and they still had not secured all of the staffing they required.

(Author's Note: Tommy Drew-Brook was hand picked by William Stephenson, head of the BSC, to be Director of the Canadian operations of the BSC. It was to Drew-Brook that Eric Curwain (a.k.a. Bill Simpson) reported.)

Bill Hardcastle entered the Royal York and proceeded to the cafe. He was just about to ask the waitress if she had seen a man fitting a particular description when a man of about forty years of age came up to him and introduced himself as Tommy, just Tommy.

After they sat down, they ordered coffee and entered into some light conversation. Bill told Tommy that he was living with his parents and that he was concerned about their ability to look after themselves. Tommy told him not to worry, that his folks would be taken care of. Ultimately, they were provided for by the Government and Bill received a good wage. Several times during their conversation, Tommy said to him, "We shall continue if you are still interested. "Tommy told Bill that he would be "fairly independent in this work" and that the work was very important. He told him that he would be taken to a camp where he would be trained in taking care of himself. "This is wartime," he said, and he told Bill that he "liked all of his men and women to be trained for any eventuality."

(Author's Note: In fact it was obligatory that all camp personnel, regardless of gender, be able to complete the courses given at the camp. The staff had to take the training because if there were an attack on the Camp by commandos, every man and woman had to be qualified to defend themselves and the Camp at any cost.)

Tommy asked Bill if he could "recommend anyone else" for his staff and Bill inquired as to how his own name had been proposed. Naturally,

Tommy declined to tell him. Bill told him that a friend of his, Hughey Durrant, was also an excellent Ham and that Hughey "had just been married." As a matter of course, they did not want married men for the program, but "exceptions were made" and the Government looked after the wives very well in those cases. It occurred to Bill that Tommy had most likely heard of him through other Hams.

(Author's Note: Indeed, when Bill got to the Camp, he was surprised to find that he already knew some of the men there.)

In the days to follow, Bill received a letter from the BSC headquarters in New York City." It merely stated that he had been *'signed on'* and gave him his starting salary, confirming his recruitment, and advised that he could be let go at any time if he was not performing satisfactorily. Bill received his "security clearance — 'Top Secret'."

"About a month passed before Bill actually went to the Camp. The pay began immediately while he was still at the Star, and he was able to gather some money together to purchase a house. Houses were inexpensive relative to salary in those days. The day Bill left the paper Tait said, 'I hear you are about to do some important war work.' Bill wondered just what Tait had been told regarding his departure, but was given the usual severance pay and he never returned to the Star."

A few days after leaving his position at the newspaper, Bill was told to go to a previously arranged location at the "Royal York between 8:00 and 9:00 on the morning of April 5 ,1942. He had said goodbye to his parents, unable to tell them of his destination." Bill and "six others were there in the suite, including Hughey Durrant, the Ham that Bill had recommended for the program, and a man named Bernie Sandbrook who would later become Bill's best friend. There were two fellows from Montreal, one named George, and an Eric Adams." They had three Georges at Camp X so they called this one "George the First." The group had been told that their "destination was east of Toronto." The driver started out in an army station wagon and "traveled east on the Old King's Highway # 2," constantly checking "in his rear view mirror." He stopped at the top of Thornton Road, the entrance to Camp X, to see if they were being followed. He actually got out of the car, walked around it, kicked the tires, and then jumped back in and drove down Thornton Road "like a bat out of hell!"

(Author's Note: Standing orders stated that, to avoid detection, when driving back to the Camp with a dignitary or even just with supplies, you were never to turn down Thorton Road if there were another car in sight. You were to continue on and later turn around and try again.)

As they raced down Thornton Road, all Bill could see were open fields, cattle and horses. Closer to the lake, he saw a simple sign on a post, "Prohibited Area, Department of National Defence." They turned on to a smaller road, passing an apple orchard off to the left. It seemed to be just another farm that they were visiting. He looked ahead and thought to himself, "What are all these buildings doing out in the middle of nowhere?" Once inside, they were greeted "very cordially and were treated like officers" but the guards were not allowed to talk with them. They were shown to their quarters in the officers' building. Bill recalled, upon entering, that the door to his room had bullet holes in it. When he inquired what had happened, he was told, "Don't let it bother you. Some of the guys were just fooling around."

18. Major Skilbeck, centre, with his Canadian Team at Camp X, 1943

"One of the instructors took them under his wing and made them feel quite comfortable." Their single nine by nine foot rooms were very well appointed with comfortable furniture; "a desk, a bed, a lamp and a chair." At the administration building, they were introduced to the Camp Adjutant-Quartermaster Bushell who welcomed them and answered their questions regarding the Camp. "Bushell" told them that they would be issued uniforms, military in style, but with no badges nor insignia. The Captain asked Bill to sign for his supplies, and just as he was about to do so, the Captain added, "Oh, just Bill would be sufficient, or Yorkie if you prefer." Bill did not know how the Captain knew that his nickname was 'Yorkie,' but he was learning that it did no good to ask.

Mac McDonald recalls that someone made a mistake in furnishing the

NCO's quarters. The furniture came from Simpson's Department Store in Toronto. Mac and Adjutant-Quartermaster Bushell were inspecting the NCO's quarters where Mac would be housed. Mac's mouth fell open as he took in the beautiful beds with their high bedposts, luxurious mattresses, silk pillow cases and sheets, and towels still in the cellophane packaging. Mac thought to himself that there was something funny going on. This just was not right!

Bushell asked Mac, "Well, what do you think?"

Mac replied, "I don't know, Sir. We're going to pay for this somehow. This looks too good to be true, considering that I just came from a steel bunk bed with only a single cover at the Horse Palace."

Sure enough, a week later all of it was removed and replaced with the old familiar military bunk beds.

* * *

That night, after a relaxing evening, Bill Hardcastle decided to settle in for the night. He was comfortable in his new quarters, but with the unfamiliar sounds and the new bed, he found himself tossing and turning.

Finally, Bill gave in to his restlessness, got out of bed and wandered to the window. He could see a flickering through the glass and wondered what it could be. Perhaps, given his new surroundings, it might be something that he would just have to get used to.

As he opened his door, he could smell smoke and when he looked down the hall he could see more flickering light coming from the mess. Fire! Not knowing what to do, Bill ran across the hall to the first door that he saw and pounded on it until he heard a loud yell from within, " Go to hell, can't you see I'm sleeping!" Bill forced the door open and could see Major Fred Milner lying in bed.

Bill said, " Oh!, Well look at this!"

Major Milner jumped out of bed and ran to the hall. He took one look and, given his knowledge of the layout of the building, realized immediately that they were trapped. By now, smoke had completely filled the hallway and flames could be seen getting closer. Having no other way out, Major Milner picked up his desk in an adrenaline rush and hurled it through the glass window. Both men climbed through the broken glass to freedom and safety, then ran around waking others as quickly as possible.

At the same time that Bill Hardcastle was attempting to get out of the building with Captain Milner, Mac McDonald was in his quarters when he was awakened by the disturbance. Mac jumped up and ran over to the building that was on fire and started banging on doors.

As he opened the door where Paddy Adams was asleep, Mac received the same welcome as had Bill Hardcastle.

"Go on get out of here and stop your fooling around!" said Paddy.

Mac yelled, "Get up Sir, the place is on fire!"

Paddy was still in a stupor so Mac grabbed Paddy's blanket and took everything that was in Paddy's top drawer and wrapped it in the blanket and threw it out the window to de Rewelyskow who was standing outside.

Mac went back out into the hall and ran along until he saw someone in a room, fumbling about. The smoke was thick now and it was becoming impossible to see or breathe. Mac ran into the room and could barely make out that it was Major Fairbairn who was trying to collect his valuables. He would not leave without them. The fire was now licking at the window as it spread along the exterior. Mac yelled, "Come on, Sir, leave that stuff. Let's get out of here. Now!"

Fairbairn still would not move. Mac opened the window and yelled for de Rewelyskow who came running over. Mac said, "George, you'd better come in. I can't get him out!" De Rewelyskow came in through the window with the flames at his side and together the two men got Fairbairn out of the building.

Major Fairbairn lost all of his personal effects in the fire. The building had been constructed completely of wood and it took only moments for it to burn to the ground.

The only casualty was Lieutenant-Colonel Roper-Caldbeck's dog, Bessie.

Was the fire an accident or an act of sabotage?

* * *

Bill made some fast and lasting friendships in those first days at the Camp. That is when he met Bernie (Sandbrook). Bill also discovered at that time that he had been one of the first hired.

The officers wasted no time in getting the agents started with physical training as they had a very tight schedule to follow. "The first half of the day was devoted to unarmed combat and the afternoons were spent bringing their code up to speed." Individual personalities began to unfold. "Eric Adams, a writer from Toronto, had a great sense of humour and often joked about the secrecy at Camp X."

"Little George, a bank clerk, had been brought in to look after the money. He was very nervous, especially around de Rewelyskow, the small arms expert who was also a champion wrestler from England." De Rewelyskow would go on to teach the trainees that when you come up on a man with a gun in your hand, you do not put the gun up against the man's back because he can feel it and know how close you are. You should always stand about a yard behind him. Not a useless bit of information for a bank clerk to know!

Chapter II

The Background

Jim Reese and his girlfriend Kim were out joy riding in Jim's father's 1938 Buick. It was a beautiful summer day so they had decided to go for a drive down to the beach and perhaps do a little "skinny dipping." They were heading south on Thornton Road, approaching the lake, when suddenly an army Jeep carrying two soldiers with rifles aimed cut across in front of them causing Jim to slam his foot on the brakes. Jim and Kim were taken totally by surprise. Although Canada was officially at war, Canadians did not really feel the effect other than their fathers, mothers, sons and daughters being sent overseas on a regular basis. Thus, to be confronted by two soldiers with rifles drawn was quite alarming.

The soldiers asked the obvious, "What do you think you are doing here?"

They replied, "Going for a swim."

"Not here", said the soldiers and told the kids to turn around and never come back. The soldiers did not explain that this was a Canadian Army base or a top secret installation! There were only small Department of National Defence signs posted to indicate that this was in any way a restricted area and, contrary to folklore, only the original four-foot barbed wire fences which had been used for keeping the cattle inside the property when it was the farm known as 'Glenrath'. The higher eight-foot barbed wire fences did not appear until 1946 when Camp X was turned over to the Canadian Signal Corps. Camp X was so secret that it could not risk putting up any "red flags" which would lead to its discovery.

Camp X was protected solely by a grid of roads that criss-crossed through the rolling fields and was patrolled, twenty four hours a day, by Jeep. By keeping the original farmhouses, barns, and other outbuildings intact, and with no signs or fences, the Camp would appear inconspicuous.

One night, while Mac McDonald and Alex McInnis were on duty together in the guard house on Thorton Road, a car came down the road and drove straight past them. It is likely that the occupants of the car might not have even seen the guard house as it was covered by brush and Mac always kept the interior lights out to make it easier for him to detect any type of movement outside.

Mac turned to Alex and said, "Let's see what they're up to." The two of them started walking down Thornton Road toward the lake where the car had stopped. There were four occupants in the car, a young man and a young woman in the front seat, and the same in the back.

Mac said to Alex, "You take the other side."

As Alex walked to the far side of the car, Mac drew his forty-five from its holster and approached the driver's side. He tapped on the window. The driver rolled down the window and asked Mac what he wanted.

Mac Said, "Didn't you see the sign at the top of the road, 'Restricted Area, Keep Out?' "

The fellow replied, "Yes, I saw it, but that doesn't mean anything."

Mac answered, "I've got news for you, it does mean something. You had better start your car, turn around, head back to where you came from and don't come back here again."

The fellow, with some misdirected sense of bravado in front of his friends, began to give Mac a hard time. "You don't have any authority here. Let me see your authority." Mac took his flashlight and shone it on his other hand where everyone in the car could now see the forty-five as bright as day.

Mac simply said, "This is my authority!"

The two girls began to cry hysterically and the driver started the car, spun around and drove back up Thorton Road, leaving Mac and Alex in a cloud of dust.

* * *

Early on in my investigation of Camp X, I was told that the buildings were erected by the Corps of Engineers. A while later, I found that everything related to the Camp was, in fact, created through "a friend", or "a friend of a friend." Eric Curwain told me that a local contractor, "a friend," built the Camp.

By keeping every aspect of the Camp in a closed inner circle, the BSC were able to control who knew what about the Camp and to keep a tight reign on secrecy, not unlike the purchase of the Camp property, which, of course, was all handled by "a friend of a friend." To my knowledge, the Police Department, the Fire Department, the Army, even the RCMP, were not allowed into the Camp. It didn't matter how much they tried, no one was admitted unless invited.

Everything related to the Camp had to be kept a secret. If you entered the Camp, you had to swear an oath of secrecy under the 'Official Secrets Act.'

* * *

There was an obvious and logical barrier between the Camp and the rest of Whitby. To the north of the Camp was the Canadian Pacific Railway line that ran parallel to the lake making it easy to guard from there toward the south as the land sloped toward the lake and an open horizon.

Looking northward from the Camp, nothing could be seen beyond the Canadian Pacific line as it was elevated at least twenty feet. There were only two single-lane tunnels, or culverts, cutting through the C.P. line; one at what is now Thornton Road and the other further west at a side road. Any unsuspecting person approaching the C.P. line driving south toward the lake would enter one of the tunnels and, immediately upon exiting, would be on Camp property only to find himself looking down the barrel of a rifle.

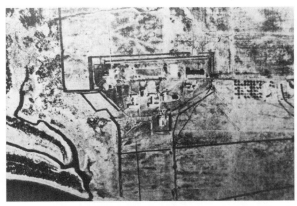

19. An aerial photograph of the Camp taken from the south and looking directly northward can better illustrate the key surrounding highlights.

1-Lake Ontario, at the bottom left hand corner, spans straight across for thirty miles, at which point it becomes the north shore of Rochester, New York.

2- Corbett Creek can be seen to the left (west) as it winds its way down toward Lake Ontario.

3- The grid of roadway protecting the perimeter of the Camp can be seen as it branches out from the Camp.

4- Directly north and out of the picture is the Canadian Pacific high line and, north of that, George Allin's farm. Even further north one would run straight into the King's Highway # 2.

5- To the right of the picture (east) and just beyond the apple orchard as seen in the picture, is Thorton Road, the main entrance to Camp X. Thornton Road is also the boundary line between Whitby and Oshawa. The property on the other side of Thorton Road (east) was owned and farmed by George Allin's brother. There the two men, while tilling their land, would watch some of the agents-in-training across the open fields.

6- Further to the right (east) and out of the picture was the Oshawa General Motors Plant which bordered the Allin farm.

* * *

George Glenn Allin farmed the adjacent property just north of the Camp all through the war years but never knew exactly what went on "down there" until well after the war. He had an understanding with the Camp officers that, as long as he stayed on his side of the railway tracks, they would remain "friends."

20. Agents practice being interrogated.
Note the Canadian Pacific Rail Line in the background

One day, George was out tending to his cattle and discovered that one of his cows had wandered away and through the tunnel. George naturally decided to go looking for her. He recalled his instruction to stay north of the tracks, but it was wartime and he needed to account for all of his cattle at all times. After all, cattle meant money.

George drove his tractor through the tunnel and came out the other side looking for his wandering cow. Within minutes a Jeep pulled up in front of him with a uniformed soldier pointing a rifle at him. The guard recognized George immediately and said, "You know that I have orders to shoot to kill".

George answered, "Well then you had better get on with it because I've come for my cow and I'm not leaving without her!"

"All right, get her and hurry up about it." George left *with* his cow and headed back through the tunnel.

Eveline Jane Allin, George's wife, was sitting in her favourite rocking chair on her front porch one warm summer evening while George was in the house taking a nap. As she looked off to her left she could see that the sun was just going down and there was the most beautiful sunset.

Three men walked around the corner of the old farmhouse and greeted her in a foreign accent. Eveline returned their greeting. The men said that they were from the "farm" down by the lake and that they had friends who had been to the Allin farm previously. Their friends had told them that when they got to the farm, they should look up Mrs. Allin as they had often visited the old farmhouse and had sat and talked with Mr. And Mrs. Allin for hours.

"Can I get you boys a cup of tea?," Eveline asked.

The men answered in their broken English, "Oh yes, please!"

This visit was not a surprise at all to Eveline. It had become customary for agents to make the trip up the road to visit on her front porch and have tea and biscuits with her and her husband. In fact, she looked forward to hearing the different stories of their homelands and all about their families. It became a routine that every Saturday night Eveline Allin could expect someone to come around that corner shortly after dinner.

* * *

In 1977, Alan Longfield and I had the privilege of interviewing Tommy Drew-Brook (head of the BSC in Canada) and his lovely wife, Mabel, at their apartment in Toronto. Ironically, this was Tommy's last interview as he died just six days later. During this interview, Tommy reflected on his commitment to (Sir) William (Bill) Stephenson, originating when they had served together during World War I, and of his involvement with the BSC.

"Bill and I were great friends. We flew together in the same squadron (No. 73 squadron of the Royal Flying Corps). He was a damn good flier..... We kept in touch between the wars, of course, and when Bill came out to Canada in 1940, he came to see me. By then Bill's operation (BSC) had grown enormously... He wanted to retain someone in Canada because he needed a base in a country that was at war and was close to the United States and South America, where he had many operations. Charles Vining (the first head of the Canadian BSC operations), a great friend of mine, and I, decided to sign on and give Bill a hand."

Vining and Drew-Brook were in the forefront of many hundreds of Canadians who were to become involved in the BSC's extensive operations in New York, Toronto and Camp X. In Drew-Brook's words, "the Canadian contribution was perfectly wonderful". Drew-Brook himself, a brilliantly successful Toronto investment broker, was entitled "to sit this one out", having sustained a severe back injury as the result of an air crash in 1918. Instead, and in spite of the pain and suffering that resulted from his previous injury, this outwardly modest man dedicated his enormous organizational talents and creativity to assist in the establishment of (Sir) William Stephenson's Canadian base.

The administrative headquarters for the BSC's Canadian operations was established in a suite in the prestigious Toronto head office building of the Canadian Bank of Commerce. Using the greatest discretion, Drew-Brook, with Vining's assistance, established this operational base "with the utmost co-operation of the Canadian government and the RCMP." From this base, and utilizing Drew-Brook's and Vining's extensive connections within the

Toronto business community, an ever expanding range of espionage and counter-espionage activities were planned and executed. An early task, in Drew-Brook's words, was "to locate, appraise and purchase a property to meet (Sir) William Stephenson's very special requirements".

Drew-Brook and Vining were advised by Stephenson's couriers from Manhattan that the clandestine working site must combine diverse topographic and climatic features including ease of security, suitability for "special" training operations and long distance radio installations, as well as accessibility from BSC Headquarters in New York. A number of Canadian locations were considered. Decisive in the final choice were recommendations made by communications experts from the University of Toronto who settled on an isolated stretch of farm land located on the north shore of Lake Ontario between the City of Oshawa and the Town of Whitby. Drew-Brook and Vining had found Camp X, which was to be, in (Sir) William Stephenson's words, "the clenched fist preparing for the knock out".

By January of 1941, William Stephenson was so desperate to find qualified women for his operation in New York that he instructed Tommy Drew-Brook to place an advertisement in the Toronto Telegram;

> *Wanted!*
> *Women for Specialized military work*
> *Apply;*
> *Mr. Bill Simpson*
> *25 King St.*
> *Toronto, Ontario*

From this single advertisement, the British Security Co-Ordination hired seven hundred women, each one interviewed and screened by the RCMP. Upon acceptance, all the women were sent to Manhattan.

Mrs. Elma Fleming of Toronto, one of the recruits from this advertisement, went on to become William Stephenson's personal secretary. It was Mrs. Fleming who would later type out the official British Security Co-Ordination history from the personal files of Sir William Stephenson in 1946.

Sir William Stephenson's personal advocacy of the development of specialized arsenal and unusual strategies as proposed by Winston Churchill produced an extensive research and development branch in Canada. With overall control resting in the BSC's headquarters in New York and local operational control resting in Toronto, Camp X was to become the principal research facility for the entire network.

"Development of new forms of plastique explosives were perfected and tested at the Camp under the direction of research teams headed by experts from the University of Toronto. The resultant explosive, RDX, had such diverse capability that its use (attached to the exhaust system of an aircraft, for example), caused many leading Nazis to fear flying even from supposedly secure installations. The explosives were so refined that, in the event of an emergency, they could be swallowed provided that the assistance of a physician could be obtained within a few hours time."

Working closely with Camp X, an extensive network, known as "Station M" was developed and based in Toronto in order to forge papers and documents and to secure all other things necessary for operatives destined for occupied territory.

"As a secure site and with easy access to the United States, the Camp provided an ideal meeting place when the necessity arose for consultation among the higher levels of espionage agencies. On numerous occasions, personnel at the Oshawa airport were shuffled into hangars as American State Department aircraft landed at the airport and unloaded their secret passengers. Known to have visited the Camp in this fashion were 'Wild Bill' Donovan, who became head of the wartime American OSS, and J. Edgar Hoover, legendary head of the FBI. Over the course of the war, many distinguished persons would visit Camp X for one reason or another, likely as not in the middle of the night to avoid detection. It is, of course, a matter of record that Ian Fleming trained here and, from his experience, would garner the knowledge to later write the *James Bond* novels."

* * *

The Sinclair Farm "Glenrath", in 1940, was the home of the late Robert Sinclair. It was a magnificent country retreat featuring a large farmhouse with eight bedrooms, parlour, living room, spacious country-style kitchen, two large barns, fieldstone root cellar and deep artesian wells.

21. The Sinclair homestead, "Glenrath," Circa 1905

The property, consisting of two-hundred and seventy-five secluded acres, was ideally suited for the BSC's requirements. It was private with dense stands of chestnut trees and bush providing both a northern windbreak and a privacy barrier. It was accessible from Lake Ontario with a commanding lakefront vista of majestic shoreline bluffs and a broad sandy beach. It was also reasonably close to both Toronto for logistical and tactical support, and to Oshawa for rest and recreation, yet sufficiently isolated for effective security.

Through a nominee, in order to avoid suspicion, Drew-Brook quietly assembled this and neighbouring properties. It is recorded that the Sinclair land was sold, "at a low price ($12,000), personally provided by (Sir) William Stephenson, to a stranger". Stephenson's trust and sense of urgency had been fully repaid by Drew-Brook in one masterful and complex maneuver.

William Gladstone Sinclair was born near Biggar, Lanarkshire, Scotland, on July 11, 1810. In 1833, he married Margaret Prentice and sailed to Canada where he settled in Whitby township near the farm of a friend from the old country, James Tweedy.

For some years after his arrival, Mr. Sinclair hired himself out as a labourer at various farms in Whitby. For fourteen years he rented a farm near Almonds at the west end of the township. In 1861, Mr. Sinclair purchased "Lot #18 broken front concession", east of Corbett Creek, where he established a large farm he called "Glenrath".

He built a grand country house where the Sinclairs raised twelve children, seven daughters and five sons. They also had fourteen grandchildren and seven great-grandchildren at the time of William Sinclair's death at the age of 88 on June 30, 1899.

Shortly before Mrs. Sinclair's death in 1893, the couple celebrated their sixtieth wedding anniversary. The Sinclair family was well known and quite prominent in Whitby's history. John Sinclair, the third child and second son, farmed on "Lot 24, concession 4" of Whitby township and donated the land for the Sinclair school which was still operating as of 1979. The brick school house was build in 1874.

William Sinclair, known as W. E. N. Sinclair, a son of John Sinclair, was a well known Oshawa lawyer who became the youngest mayor of that city. He entered provincial politics and, during the 1920's, was the leader of the Ontario Liberal Party in the legislature. At the time of his death, he was a Liberal member for Ontario riding in the Mackenzie King government.

The original William Sinclair who settled in Whitby in 1833 was a staunch Reformer (Liberal) and was a reader of the Toronto Globe, George Brown's Liberal newspaper since its founding in 1844. One can only imagine what William Sinclair would think if he had had the foresight to see what would become of his beloved 'Glenrath' in 1942.

The Sinclairs were devout Presbyterians and, when there was a disruption in the church in 1843, William Sinclair joined the Free Church Party. William Sinclair's son John, became an elder in the Free Church. One of John's sons, Norman, became a Presbyterian minister, and was honoured as moderator of the SYNOD of Toronto and Kingston.

The last of William Sinclair's children, Alex Sinclair, died in 1934 at the age of 80. His nephew, Robert Bravener, operated the original Glenrath farm from about 1910 to 1935. It then passed into the Sinclair estate which was acquired by the BSC as the sight of Camp X.

22. An unknown fireman watches the Sinclair house
burn to the ground, 1964

We are told that all that remains of the original homestead are two brown porcelain door knobs given to members of the Sinclair family by the Commander of the Camp before the house was destroyed in 1964 by the Whitby fire Department as part of their on-going training.

* * *

In 1942, were you to take a walk through the Camp and buildings, you would start at Thornton Road. Here you would find a wooden sign nailed to an old and weathered post about four feet high. The sign simply announced, "Prohibited Area - Department of National Defence." From this point, you would walk westward along the original farm road into "Glenrath". The road was a typical country gravel road about ten feet wide. You would have to pass a small unassuming guardhouse with a swing gate beyond which no one proceeded without proper orders. This was the only gate to the Camp.

*23. This unassuming sign is the only one to greet you from
Thorton Road turning into Camp X*

Approximately three hundred feet from Thornton Road and to the left would be the old original apple orchard. Directly south of that, as you looked toward Lake Ontario, you would be able to see the "giant Rhombic Antennae which could originate or pluck coded Morse traffic from the ionosphere."

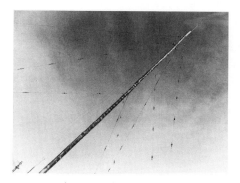

24. The giant Rhombic Antennae

25. A field full of Rhombic Antennae

26. The comfortably appointed parlour of the Commandant's Quarters

About another one hundred feet further along the gravel road, if you were again to look to the left, you would see the Commandant's Quarters behind the tall chestnut trees which lined both sides of the road. The Commandant's Quarters was certainly a house of luxury. As you entered it, you would find a comfortable living room with plush furniture. At the back of the house was the Commandant's bedroom. There was no kitchen as the Commandant ate in the officers' mess with the other officers. Off to the right of the living room was a private parlour shut off from the rest of the house by a single closed door. It was in this room that all of the top secret, confidential decision making meetings were held. It was also in this room that such people as Sir William Stephenson (BSC), J. Edgar Hoover (FBI), Samuel McLaughlin (General Motors), Inspector George McClellan (RCMP), "Wild Bill" William Donavon (OSS), and many others were entertained.

27. Communications building (left) and Commandant's Quarters (right)

Directly across the road from the Commandant's Quarters was the Communications Building, a bustling hub of activity and secrecy. One woman who worked in the Communications building said that "no one ever knew what anyone else's job was because we were never allowed to discuss the Camp with each other. It was all on a first name basis and no one ever knew the other's last name."

Even employees were not allowed to drive their own vehicles into the Camp. They were picked up at their homes by a driver and driven back home again at the end of the shift. Rarely did anyone enter the Camp who was not being driven by a Camp chauffeur. This was one way of ensuring that no person or artifact of any kind could be smuggled into or out of the Camp without the guard's knowledge.

28. Mac McDonald on duty in the guardhouse

Long shifts were the norm for Camp X employees. It was not unusual to work a six-day week with twelve hour shifts making any form of social life nearly non-existent. Although, says one woman, "We did occasionally have the odd party."

The Communications Building contained some of the most sophisticated equipment available. So extensive were the BSC's communications requirements that, in addition to the transmitting and receiving capabilities of the Camp X network, British Security were to require cable capacity costing in excess of one million dollars, an exorbitant figure in the early 1940's.

Looking inside the Communications Building, you would see a number of women hunched over teletype machines creating miles of ribbons of coded and decoded messages. This bustling beehive housed a never ending exercise and grew larger and larger as the war years went on.

29. left & 30. right. At work in the communications building

31. Camp X, 1956

As one can see in a photograph taken of the Camp in 1956, the Camp itself then remained basically as it was during the war with the exception of the new 'Hydra' building built after the war when, in 1946, the Canadian Corps of Signal took over the installation. With the invention of new, more powerful equipment, it quickly became apparent that the old 'Hydra' building just would not suffice, so the Signal Corps had this new, much larger building built. Note the location of the General Motors facility to the northeast.

Directly west of the Communications Building was the Jump Tower. Parachute jumping was a mandatory part of the regimen for most agents-in-training going through Camp X. As at least one agent would say after the war, " It was enough to scare the hell out of you".

32. The ninety-foot tall jump tower

As you passed by the ninety foot tall Jump Tower and continued your walk westward, you would now see the other buildings coming into view. First was 'Hydra' as you looked left and southward toward the lake.

"Hydra, the short wave (15 MHz) transmitter/receiver with its massive Rhombic Antennae in the background, was inconspicuously housed in nothing more than a wooden shed. Cover for the sudden emergence of the antennae was provided by the Canadian Broadcasting Corporation's continuing efforts to serve local subscribers."

33. Hydra-note living quarters tent (right) used after the fire

Entering Hydra required the opening of one of two very large doors that went from the floor to the ceiling, designed purposely to facilitate the movement of large equipment in and out of Hydra. The building had windows all around placed seven feet up from the floor in order to be out of reach of snooping eyes.

Once inside Hydra, you would note that it looked like any other component shop with radio equipment and accessories everywhere. Over in one corner were large crates of Ozopure, the cooling liquid that was used to cool the gigantic tubes required to run the transmitters.

In behind Hydra was a building which housed the boiler room and the shop. Like most military establishments in the forties, the buildings of Camp X were linked together by a series of underground tunnels which supplied the heating system for the entire Camp. These tunnels were covered by a catwalk network of heavy boards so that maintenance workers could have easy access to the tunnels in the event of a problem. After the war, the stories which emerged telling of secret tunnels linking building to building with dispatchers running top secret messages to and from Hydra to the C.O. were nothing more than a figment of someone's overactive imagination. As mentioned previously, the Camp was so cunningly set up that to have a man in uniform walk from Hydra to the Communications Building with a piece of paper in his hand would not cause anyone any more suspicion than seeing someone walk down the street with a newspaper in hand.

Directly behind Hydra, the Camp had its own excellent repair shop. For obvious reasons of security, no one entered or left the Camp unless it were absolutely essential. All repairs were done inside the Camp by Camp personnel who were assigned full time to maintaining the Camp in top operating condition.

34. Camp X was totally self-sufficient with its own repair shop (left) and steam heating system 35 (right).

36. The Lecture hall

The next building on your tour would be the Lecture Hall. As the sign on the inside of the door said, "Know Your Enemy". The Lecture Hall was complete with a classroom for blackboard theory, a library of military books from all ages, spy books both fictional and factual, and a special room full of enemy uniforms, regalia, and weaponry of the Axis forces, including all ranks of the German armed forces. Other features of the building included facilities for the extensive planning and rehearsing of "Special Operations". Material and supplies were collected from all over North America to assist in mounting realistic simulations of proposed clandestine operations.

If you were to continue the walk westward, again off to the left and behind the Lecture Hall stood the two 'H' buildings, identical in size and at opposites to each other. These building were built to house the Officers, N.C.O.'s, other personnel and agents-in-training. Each man had his own room of approximately eight feet by nine feet, appointed with a comfortable bed, a dresser, and a desk and chair.

37. Bill Hardcastle (far left) in the mess hall

During Ontario's cold harsh winters, it was a pleasant relief to get up in the morning, walk down the hall to the mess for breakfast, and not have to endure the elements outside. Barracks were at each end of both buildings with a large mess in the middle. Of course the Officers ate in their mess and the N.C.O.'s and other personnel ate in theirs. Eating hours were staggered so that the agents would not have contact with unauthorized personnel. Each building contained a completely equipped kitchen able to feed two hundred people each three times a day.

38. Looking north from the lake with Camp X on the horizon, 1942

The only difference between the two buildings was that the one on the southwest side had a basement which had been converted to an underground firing range. The ground outside had a natural steep slope which made it perfect for the creation of a hidden bunker, the back wall of which was made of half inch solid steel plating.

Approaching the east side of the Camp which runs parallel to Corbett Creek was the old Sinclair farmhouse as well as a large barn, a smaller barn and an outside root cellar. An artesian well finished off the beautiful country farm and made it a great sight to start building a 'Special Training School'.

Continuing the walk southward with the two 'H' buildings on either side of you, you would now see the entire vista of Lake Ontario unobstructed by any other buildings. Only lovely open grassy fields sloped gradually toward the lake, yet some three hundred feet away. Even more training took place on these fields; night time assault training from the shore of the lake, explosives training under water, and cliff climbing with ropes and bearing heavy back packs. Your walking tour ends at the top of these cliffs where the road ended abruptly and dropped sharply down thirty feet to the water.

The Camp X training staff, in fact, took full advantage of every square inch of Camp X. There was not a piece of the property that was not used for some type of training, a glowing tribute to the brilliant training staff.

39. Aerial view of Camp X, 1968

In this aerial photograph of Camp X taken in 1968, please note a number of significant features. All of the original buildings remained at that time with the addition of the new 'Hydra' building at the lower part of the picture. Also, note the cleared area around the Camp which served as a security area with an eight foot high barbed wire fence around the perimeter. Although this picture was taken twenty three years after the war ended, the beach area is totally undisturbed, as it remains today, with thirty foot high bluffs which had been used to train the agents in the art of secretly infiltrating the enemy target from a beachhead.

Just up from the beach you will note dark circular patches of ground. These are the scars which remain where the explosives training took place. When the author visited the Camp in 1977, these pock-marked areas were still quite visible.

* * *

As noted previously, there were other peripheral entities that played an important role in establishing the exact location for Camp X. Logistically significant features such as the situation of the German Officers' POW Camp at Bowmanville, and the Oshawa Airport, both located within twenty five miles of Camp X, will be addressed later as their connection to the Camp is revealed. First of all, I would like to delve into the importance of Defence Industries Limited.

Prior to the war, the town of Ajax did not exist. There were simply miles of rolling hills and open farm land with the occasional farm house sprinkled here and there, much like the one at Camp X. At the outbreak of hostilities and with Canada's entry into the war, there was a rapidly growing need for munitions plants. What is now the town of Ajax on the outskirts of

Toronto was a prime location for establishing one of these plants.

The Canadian military called upon the Canadian Industries Limited (CIL) for their co-operation and the name became DIL, or Defence Industries Limited. That was the official name of Ajax during the Second World War. The town of Oshawa, particularly because of the Oshawa motor works situated there, was called upon for many of the personnel who would subsequently work at DIL. Many of the men were already working at the General Motors plant so their wives were recruited to go to work for DIL.

40. The main entrances, both vehicular and pedestrian, to DIL, as well as the bus depot to the right

As the munitions manufacturing plants began to push up across the farm land, there grew a necessity for short term housing. What are now called "war homes" were erected in a controlled fashion. Were you to travel to Ajax today, you would see hundreds of these war homes, all strategically placed just outside what was the entrance gate to DIL on the north side of the 401 Highway starting at Harwood Ave. Although the houses were small and inexpensive to build, usually with no garage, they were, in fact, well constructed. The instantly constructed town consisted of war munitions plants, homes, stores, schools, churches, community halls, and a post office, everything a small town would need.

The author actually worked in the town of Ajax as a young boy in what was then Bassin's Food Market and I can still recall to this day the sirens going off at noon. They were originally air raid sirens but, at that time, they signified to the workers that it was lunch time. For many years the siren continued to be sounded at 12:00 noon. It also sounded again at 9:00 p.m. to signal curfew. Anyone under sixteen had to be at home or have a very good reason for being out that late.

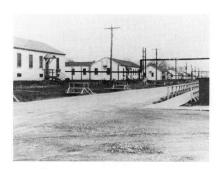

*41. The female employees' residences at DIL, each of the twenty buildings
contained fifty rooms and housed 100 women.*

One thing that really fascinated me at the time was that the entire town was heated by one source, a steam plant powerhouse. The entire (approximately) three thousand acres of DIL were heated by an underground system of ductwork originating at the power house, connecting all of the buildings over the entire area, and then returning back to the source of the steam plant. It is amazing that, to this day, many buildings are still heated from that original steam plant.

It soon became apparent that the local population was not large enough to support both General Motors and Defence Industries Ltd., so an appeal was sent out across Canada. Advertisements were placed in all the local papers in the smaller towns in northern Ontario, as well as in other provinces, offering a lucrative opportunity for people to live and work. The town quickly established a bus system for the workers. Buses would pick them up at their residences to transport them to DIL where they were required to produce name tags as proof of identification. The rate of pay was approximately 50 cents an hour, an excellent wage during World War II.

Security was extremely tight at DIL. There was even an elaborate system to illuminate the entire area at night giving it a daylight effect and there were eight foot barbed wire fences surrounding the entire area of the plant. Safety was one of the highest concerns. When a worker first came to DIL he or she was required to take a safety course which had to be completed successfully before the worker could be assigned to a work station on the assembly line. So safety conscious were they that even smoking was banned. There was a penalty of imprisonment if you were caught with matches or a lighter, and cigarettes were not allowed anywhere inside the munitions factory area.

The normal weekly shift consisted of six days, eight hours per day. There were three shifts each day and a worker was on a two week swing. The plant was closed on Sunday. At the height of the war, DIL employed over ten thousand people who filled over fifty million shells of every size and caliber. DIL was obviously a very convenient source of munitions used in training at Camp X.

42. Workers on the line at DIL removing shipping caps and cleaning the 3.7 shells

43. Women on the assembly line at DIL 'filling shells'

There were special training techniques which placed the agents on a mock mission to infiltrate DIL. These exercises would be pre-arranged similar to the General Motors exercises. The foreman of a particular building would be made aware that he could expect a "visitor" sometime during his shift. It then became the foreman's responsibility to be on the watch constantly and be prepared to inform the DIL guards immediately of any peculiarities. This particular exercise was beneficial to both Camp X and DIL. Depending on the success of the infiltration, the guard would alert either Camp X instructors or DIL defence managers as to what steps had to be taken in order to correct the breach. This training was taken very seriously as the outcome could be catastrophic.

Lynn-Philip Hodgson

.

Chapter III

The Agents' Recruitment and Training

Eric Curwain quietly went about his work as if it were an ordinary day. Methodically he tap, tap, tapped on the keys of his suitcase radio. As Eric continued his extremely important message, he could hear bombs blasting, now in the distance, but coming ever closer.

In actuality, there was nothing the least bit ordinary about this day. From his lair in the British Embassy in Poland, Eric Curwain was in the process of advising Britain that the German invasion of Poland was underway. Only two days hence, Britain would declare war on Germany. Upon completion of the message, Eric made his way out of Poland via Romania and Norway, then linked up with 'friends' who whisked him off to England and subsequently to his ultimate destination in Canada.

Hollywood would have us believe that every secret agent was recruited on a foggy night by a dark and dangerous 'Bogartesque' character, in trench coat and Fedora, standing in the shadow of a street lamp. A burst of flame as he strikes a match to light a cigarette, illuminating his face for a split second, serves as a signal to his contact on the next corner under his street lamp, and soon another rugged but very handsome young man disappears into the mist, only to reappear scenes later with his own trench coat. This scene may make for a dramatic and romantic moment in the movies. In reality, however, Eric's recruitment into the Secret Service was typical of that of many other young men at the time.

"As a youngster I had spent years in the Royal Air Force signals branch. On impulse therefore, that morning in 1938, at the height of Britain's between-wars somnolence, I called on my former commanding officer, wing Commander C. K. Chandler, at the Air Ministry in London. He was courteous, even remembered me, and introduced me to another officer, telling him my need. What happened in the next few minutes showed how casually the affairs of the Empire were run at that time, at least from the security angle. However, the casualness does not necessarily imply inefficiency.

"The officer picked up his telephone and spoke to someone for about two minutes. While doing so he gave me a friendly scrutiny and told his listener, 'I think so.'

"Within the week I was being interviewed by one of the few brilliant men I have known in my vagabond life. He was dark, almost swarthy, and the type that fascinates women. He was my height, about five foot eleven inches, and well built. He had retained his World War I rank of Captain but was not, at that moment, in uniform.

"In the hectic but informal months of the summer of 1938, his staff called him 'Pop' (Captain R. Gambier-Parry). Later, when he was promoted to Brigadier, his manner became less genial although his persuasiveness increased as his communications network became more and more vital to the war effort."

The next thing Eric Curwain knew, he was on a ship bound for New York and a meeting with a man named William Stephenson. Much has been written about William Stephenson, the head of the British Security Co-Ordination (BSC) which was established by Winston Churchill to oversee his North American intelligence operation. It was Churchill who gave Stephenson the code name "Intrepid", later the subject of the book by, ironically, William Stevenson, *A Man Called Intrepid,* and the subsequent movie of the same name.

Many years after the war, Eric Curwain wrote the following:

"By the time I was introduced to Bill Stephenson by Pat Bayly in 1942 I had met a number of generals and government officials of ambassadorial level but none of them impressed me as much as this 'quiet Canadian'.

"In addition to his duties as Secret Intelligence Service (SIS) Chief in America, Stephenson was also in charge of the operations of the British SOE in North America and the Balkans. There seemed to be no limit to his versatility in harassing the German and Italians wherever they operated in the western hemisphere."

In 1941, William Stephenson was invited to attend the conference between Winston Churchill and President Roosevelt which was convened on the H.M.S. Prince of Wales. On board, and under tightest security, the world leaders discussed how they would embark on a course of 'secret warfare,' as well as other critical issues.

Again, Curwain's own words:

"Our office in Toronto was connected by a permanent direct line to the downtown headquarters of Inspector (later Commissioner) George McClellan of the Royal Canadian Mounted Police.

"One nice thing about Tommy Drew-Brook (Canadian head of the British Security Co-ordination) was that he completely ignored the fact that his new civilian-dressed assistant was a mere sergeant in the Royal Corps of Signals. He gave me a generous living allowance and only asked that during off-duty hours I should be always available by telephone. He even let me choose my own 'nom-de-guerre' and as 'Bill Simpson' I began covering the waterfront in a search for radio Hams as soon as I had been introduced to Inspector McClellan.

44. George B. McClellan, the father of the modern security service in Canada

"McClellan was an understanding man and exactly my preconceived idea of a Mountie: well built, face well tanned, positive manner and always good humoured. He had served his 'apprenticeship' in the usual way, riding a horse and spanning the North West and the Arctic. He was a Westerner, as was his charming wife. He took a week off to undergo training at our Oshawa camp where all sorts of skullduggery were practiced and encouraged. McClellan enjoyed his training there and no doubt taught the Commando instructors something in return, such as the non-violent way of ejecting a violent man from a saloon: go up behind the offender, who will probably be leaning at the bar, put your right hand (or left) between his thighs from behind making him bend and try to grasp your offending fingers. But you grab his hand instead, then grip the back of his collar with your other hand and frog-march him out of the saloon. I later tried this on a paratrooper much taller than myself and found it worked."

In order to best describe some of the training, since this is still a top secret subject, I would like to borrow excerpts from a chapter of my old friend Eric Curwain's unpublished manuscript entitled, *Almost Top Secret*.

Eric Curwain was born in the university town of Cambridge, England, and studied languages there as well as in France, Germany and Spain later on. In 1918, he enlisted in the Royal Navy Volunteer Reserve as a radio operator to serve in mine-sweepers. From 1923 to 1928, he lived in France and Spain. In his youth, Curwain spent more time on sports than on studies. He won the highest awards of the Boy Scouts for endurance, high diving and boxing, and later he played four times for France in international soccer matches. In 1929, he served in the shipping offices of the Canadian International Petroleum Company in Peru and Columbia, during which time he wrote articles about the current revolutions and sold them to British publications, including *PUNCH* and London dailies.

He joined the Secret Intelligence Service (SIS) of the British Foreign Office in 1938 and served until 1946. He had experience as a Ham radio operator and was also familiar with navy, army and air force Signals procedures and he was fluent in French, Spanish and German. In his eight years in SIS, he operated in ten countries on intelligence assignments, during which time he covered the invasions of Poland and Norway, and the Russian occupation of Hungary. He served two years in Canada under William Stephenson, 'Intrepid'.

In 1946, Curwain resigned from the SIS to live in Canada. After teaching languages for a while in a Toronto private school, he took up public relations and editorial work. For ten years he edited a shipping publication with world-wide circulation. It becomes obvious why Eric Curwain was so eminently qualified for and was the natural choice to be head of the 'Canadian Division of the British Security Co-Ordination'.

Once again writing about William Stephenson, Eric Curwain continued:

45. OSS trainees at Camp X

"Camp X accepted many nationalities from diverse organizations and units, including those of the 'Office of Strategic Services'. Two OSS American trainees were sent out one day to walk the streets of Toronto and try to spread dismay and alarm among the citizens. Their orders were to do this without getting themselves arrested as Fifth Columnists, as could well happen when they were eventually let loose in Europe. It was suggested that I might like to tail them and try to catch them in 'flagrante delecto'. To help me, I took along my fourteen year old niece, Betty, who lived in Toronto and we decided we would each tail one OSS trainee.

"My American entered a barber's shop and, as soon as his turn came to sit in the chair, he began work on the man with the scissors. He met apathy and I felt frustrated for him. During his subsequent treasonable efforts that day, I followed him but cannot recall that he did any harm to Toronto's morale. But his was not an easy task and it is to be doubted that any American at that time understood the Canadian character or loyalties directing the various provinces.

"Meanwhile, my niece was seated at one end of a drug store counter farther down Jarvis Street entering in her shorthand notebook the conversation of the other OSS operator. Her notebook might one day be a valued piece of war documentation if it could be found. But the follow-up on this little episode was forgotten because one of these agents died from heart failure that evening in his hotel room."

"The men who trained for 'special duties' at the Camp would have been an elite class in any 'Foreign Legion Regiment.' They would leave Camp X as British soldiers or officers.

"Early in 1944, two men arrived. One named A.G.G. Charles De Chastelaine and the other a Romanian, George Georgescu. Both were to parachute into Romania and present Allied terms for peace to the government of that country. De Chastelaine had lived in Romania for some years and he and Georgescu knew the country's ruling clique.

"De Chastelaine was an excellent mimic and conversationalist. He accompanied me on a recruiting trip to the military camp at Niagara to interview the Commandant, Brigadier General Martin, the distinguished looking North American Indian and World War I pilot (and later a Toronto magistrate). The Brigadier and De Chastelaine got along excellently.

"Georgescu was amusing too, and an incident of his student days shows him to be also a man of initiative. Going from Romania to London to study, he decided to take along with him some Turkish liqueur and had no trouble in passing it through the customs in Europe and England using the simple strategy of putting some chicken bones in the liqueur jar and telling the customs officers at each frontier that he was a medical student taking some bone specimens to study in England. Having also a taste for bawdy classics he obtained an introduction to the British Museum Librarian and was granted permission to study the unexpurgated additions of *One Thousand and One Nights*, material he claimed was essential to his University studies concerning rare oriental perfumes.

"De Chastelaine and Georgescu were an ideal pair for their Romanian mission and it was a pity their drop into Romania was an unlucky one. The RAF pilot was out in his bearings and dropped them far from their chosen spot. They eventually landed in a Bucharest prison; the Gestapo tried to take them to Berlin but the Romanians stoutly resisted and some months later we met De Chastelaine in Bari after he and Georgescu had been released.

"Another recruit at Camp X was a Syrian called Alex whose shyness made him seem austere. By profession he was a geologist and had spent years in the United States prospecting. On completion of his training with us, we lodged him in the King Edward Hotel in Toronto and the day came when I took him his weekly living allowance, which he declined, saying he had no need for it. On my insisting, he still refused and explained: 'I understand horses and I win money at the Woodbine Race Track. I watch the horses, study their form by looking at them — not by the racing form — and back the one I fancy.'

"Our suggestion that the only men who consistently made money on track betting were syndicate operators and sometimes owners made him smile. 'But I know horses. I have studied all types of animals. I often used to see mountain lion tracks made during the night when the animals passed my bivouac, but I never worried about them. You get to know animals. They never harm you unless you annoy them. And horses well, I really know a lot about horses.'

"Marco was another recruit who refused money. As leader of one of the Yugoslav Communist groups in Toronto, he embarked at Halifax after his training, but was injured when torpedoed in the Atlantic and then returned to Toronto, where he resumed his journalistic work. My instructions were to offer him monetary compensation but this he declined; 'I did not get to Yugoslavia and do the work I was recruited for. I have no right to accept money from you.'

"To the suggestion that money might help his family, he answered: 'All my family is in Yugoslavia and I don't know which side they are fighting on.'

"After further argument he was persuaded to accept a portable typewriter. With his gray hair and stalwart figure he had a natural dignity sitting there in his not too comfortable back-room, a victim of his own strict code of ethics.

"Arnold, son of a Spanish senator, turned up at the camp for training one day, having volunteered to serve the Allies in Europe. He and his brother had engineered a beautiful coup against the Germans by organizing a big evening party on one of the Spanish islands off the west coast of Africa. While the celebrations were under way with all the port officials and police as guests, the British Navy entered the harbour and towed away some interned German merchant ships to Gibraltar — a welcome addition to the Allied merchant fleet.

" 'I can never go back home to Spain as long as Franco lives and he will never be deposed from dictatorship,' Arnold told us. This and other predictions he made about the future of Spain turned out to be correct.

"The Oshawa trainees often lapsed into more personal talks at farewell parties and sometimes the men recruited locally invited us to their homes for a last meal. One such was a Yugoslav named Paul, one of the last of the blacksmiths working in Toronto. He was preparing to drop in Yugoslavia and that final meal in his home in Toronto was, in retrospect, truly his last meal, for Paul was killed in Yugoslavia. His views on the war were simple - the Nazi doctrine was evil. He shared the same view as an unfrocked Italian priest who left the Church and his teaching profession to train with us to fight the Fascists.

"This priest, wearing civilian garb, often visited my 'branch' recruiting office on Bay Street in Toronto while awaiting shipment overseas and he was curious about my religion. I told him I enjoyed all churches, synagogues or mosques and attended any service which had music, including the Spiritualist churches. He insisted I take him to a Spiritualist service. We both dressed in ordinary city suits. The medium, holding the note case the priest had deposited on the table, said; 'This object belongs to a man, I don't know who he is but he is working in the wrong profession now. He is really a teacher and should still be teaching. I see him in, or going to, Montreal. I advise him to give up the new work he has undertaken.'

"This priest was in fact going within a few days to embark at Montreal for Europe, having finished his training at Camp X. In Italy he was killed, fighting with the partisans against Mussolini's troops.

"When I had the privilege of being invited to a banquet-style party by a big group of our Yugoslav Communist volunteers, it proved to be an emotional affair. They were of all trades; Pacific coast fishermen, Ontario miners, some woodsmen, and trappers and craftsmen. Despite my language limitation in their Slav ethnic divisions, their courtesy made me feel myself a member in good standing. Their ages ranged up to the middle forties while Marco, their leader was in his middle fifties.

"When the evening ended, the departing ones embraced the friends who had planned the evening. The Anglo-Saxon good-bye parties I had attended lacked the dignity of that Yugoslav sendoff.

"The arrival at the camp of an ebullient medical man from Brazil was yet another indication of the extent to which the war was becoming a global affair. The Brazilian was a champion high diver and judo expert in his own country and when we saw him in action on the judo mat he was as good as the instructors. He was short, thick set and quick of step and, like our agent Springbok, first and foremost a Don Juan. After seeing this handsome Brazilian throw a six-foot man across the training mat, one wondered how the ladies fared.

"It is not generally known that Brazil was already committed in several ways to helping the Allied cause. In North Africa in 1943, they had a group of skilled pilots flying Thunderbolts along side the squadrons of the U.S. Air Force. These volunteer airmen were drawing nine hundred dollars U.S. currency a month, more than the pay of an American Colonel, and their performance was outstanding. The only problem with them when they moved to Italy, said my American Air Force Colonel, was getting them out of bed in the morning, thus releasing the Italian hotel maids from concubine duties.

"Another interesting character was Rudi of Ontario, a shoemaker and Communist. To obtain a passport for him we took him to the usual firm of lawyers we consulted and asked one of the firm's partners to vouch for him. He had done this several times, but on this occasion he suggested that if someone had to perjure himself by saying he had known the applicant so many years, why not let Ottawa perjure itself?

"The lawyer's objection resulted in the insertion of the following clause on post-war applications for a Canadian passport;

> "If you were one of the persons who volunteered
> during World War II to fight in Special Forces
> overseas, state so here."

"The Toronto lawyer mentioned above said that Rudi's eloquence when denouncing the Nazi doctrine was impressive; he had not expected to find a foreign cobbler with such a command of English.

"It was a gentlemen's agreement between the Canadian government and these Special Forces operators that upon return to Canada they should be granted Canadian citizenship. I remembered this when I met Rudi in Bari, Italy, wandering around in the uniform of a sergeant-major with a back injured during parachute training in Cairo. No one in our Bari unit, to which he was now attached, knew what to do with him so I told our Colonel of the gentlemen's agreement with Ottawa and Rudi went back to Canada.

"Most of those who did their training at Oshawa, (a shoemaker, a priest, a blacksmith, a journalist, a geologist, an oil man and a Spanish aristocrat), appear to have committed their lives for an ideal. The Yugoslavs told us frankly they were not going to fight for Canada or Britain; they were at war with the Nazi and Fascists. In fairness to the Yugoslav Communists who volunteered, it should be mentioned that some of them had offered to join the Partisans even before the Russians were brought into the war by the scruff of their necks.

"The job of recruiting such men was one which inevitably engendered in the recruiter a feeling of inferiority. Sooner or later he got caught in his own net in an effort to rid himself of this feeling and I suggested to Tommy (Drew-Brook) that I should be sent as a Signal officer to work with the Partisans in Yugoslavia. A message was sent through London to Marshal Tito's headquarters in Yugoslavia, and my suggestion was accepted. With this agreed upon, I returned to England in early 1944."

One day Eric Curwain was walking through the streets of London with a young SOE recruit, Eric in civilian clothes and the recruit in uniform. They passed a staff officer on the street.

"Why didn't you salute me?" The officer asked the young SOE agent.

The agent replied, "I didn't realize that I was supposed to."

"What is your unit?" the staff officer asked.

When the young agent replied, the officer snorted, "Oh, that crowd!" as he walked away muttering to himself.

* * *

As the Camp came into full operation, it was realized that considerable manpower would be required to operate the installation effectively. An agent of Sir William Stephenson's, while in London, approached a senior officer of the Canadian Army to ask if the assistance of Canadian Army personnel could be obtained. Within twenty four hours, authorization had been received by Headquarters, Military District No. 2, in Toronto to provide one hundred and fifty army personnel, as required, for detached duty. Recruiting procedures were established by Charles Vining with the co-operation of J. L. Ralston, Minister of Defence, and the RCMP.

Carefully chosen recruits were inducted into the Canadian army with rank, uniform and concomitant pay and service benefits. As the nature of the Camp demanded flexibility, recruits were given their choice of regiments and rank was often decided by circumstances. One professor at the University of Toronto, having difficulty in dealing with his American counterparts as he officially only held the rank of Second-Lieutenant, found himself promoted to Lieutenant-Colonel overnight. A request to Sir Winston Churchill from Sir William was sufficient to have the entry made on the British regimental establishment.

The military staff headed by a succession of British commanders included four other senior British officers, and ten N.C.O. instructors. They were chosen carefully for their skills and included a former heavyweight wrestling champion of England, one of the acknowledged world experts in hand to hand combat. Others experts in explosives were so skilled in their trade that they could place a piece of shrapnel between two poles ten feet apart. Occasionally, explosives were misjudged and, on one occasion, windows were broken several miles away in neighbouring Oshawa requiring some quick cover-up work by senior Camp personnel.

Technical expertise was provided by Canadian civilians who had been quietly approached and recruited through a "word of mouth" recommendation to Drew-Brook by his talent spotters in the field. The RCMP assisted this by providing facilities and manpower without asking questions. Canadian professors of engineering, scientists, and gifted amateurs in many fields were inducted for service in the Canadian Army under the strictest rules of secrecy. Potential agents were recruited from Canada's large ethnic population to meet language and nationality requirements for projected missions. Obvious partisan sympathies, a promising psychological profile, and other factors were considered equally in the final selection and screening processes. Canada's extensive Eastern European population was a particularly fertile ground for the recruitment of potential agents.

Not always did this recruitment of the operational staff go smoothly. One day, Lieutenant-Colonel Roper-Caldbeck returned from Oshawa and, upon entering his residence, noticed that some things had been rearranged. He summoned Mac McDonald who was on guard duty that day.

"Mac, was anyone inside my residence while I was gone?," Roper-Caldbeck asked.

"Yes, Sir. Private 'T' was in there," Mac replied.

"Come with me, Mac," the CO said as the two men started to walk down the hill in search for Private 'T'.

Once he had been located, Roper-Caldbeck ordered, "Mac, escort this man to the gate and instruct him to find his way back to Military District No. 2." Once the private was gone, Roper-Caldbeck made a call to his liaison at Military District No. 2, and that was the end of Private 'T's stay at Camp X.

Typical of the BSC's recruitment procedures was the request made to a prominent Canadian union leader for help in locating potential operatives. Twenty Hungarian-born activists from the Toronto area were quickly recruited and rapidly assimilated into the Canadian Army, sent to Orillia for training, and then had their skills fine tuned by eight weeks of highly specialized training at Camp X.

The agents, after their training at Camp X, were then flown to Scotland and Egypt. Briefed, they then proceeded to Brindisi, Italy, one of the major jumping off points, and were then dropped into Eastern Europe by No. 148 Special Duty Squadron.

Not all of the recruitment and training were directed towards the European theatre. One of the most colourful groups to go through training at Camp X were the South Americans, recruited by Nelson Rockefeller, and trained to counteract Nazi sabotage plans directed again the South American rubber plantations.

During the period when Camp X was used as a commando training centre, approximately five hundred agents were trained there in any of fifty-two different courses ranging in duration from one to eight weeks. The courses, especially in the physical combat arts, were relentlessly rigorous. Instructors were often eccentric and always effective. Techniques emhasized the "make it and take it" approach to success and survival in enemy country with minimal resources available. On the Chief Instructor's door was placed the unofficial slogan of the Camp, "KNOW YOURSELF. KNOW YOUR WEAPON. KNOW YOUR ENEMY."

The Camp X 'syllabus' included the following definitions;

Terminology of Unconventional Warfare

1. Unconventional Warfare - conducted within hostile territory with predominantly indigenous forces and often with supported external sources. Considered to include these three interrelated aspects:

    1. Guerrilla Warfare, i.e. military & paramilitary operations.
    2. Evasion & Escape, i.e. movements.
    3. Subversion, i.e. undermining national strengths
       and loyalty.

    Synonyms:
    Insurgent warfare
    Irregular warfare
    Revolutionary warfare
    Guerrilla warfare

2. Guerrilla - engages in unconventional warfare. Appears in the following varieties.

    1. Partisan or patriotic
    2. Insurgent or revolutionary
    3. Urban terrorist

3. Resistance Movement-organized underground struggle within the

civil population for national liberation from military occupations.

> 1. Underground - covert organization or network seen to disrupt or overthrow an occupying military government.
> 2. Partisan - guerrilla in a narrower sense than revolutionary or insurgent guerrilla. Usually seek to restore status quo.

4. Low Intensity Conflict - encompasses all of the above.

As part of the Lecture Hall "blackboard theory", much time was spent on the importance of creating a disguise and taking on a new persona. Bill Brooker was an expert at this and after reading the following, one can see why his lectures were so much in demand.

Although the following excerpts are from the OSS, their origin is no doubt the SOE and Camp X. These pages were made available to the author through the kindness of Nathan Estey.

Now, picture yourself sitting in the Lecture Hall at Camp X, one of a dozen agents-in-training. Bill Brooker is at the lectern and is schooling you on what you need to know about disguises on your up-coming secret mission behind enemy lines. Listen intently as it could save your life!

Personal Disguise

Prepared by OSS Field Photographic Branch
for Camouflage Division

Research & Development Branch

Declassified 12-Feb.-85, CIA

First: You must study yourself and check up on your habits. Each individual has peculiar mannerisms which are characteristic of himself alone. They must be analyzed and then eliminated. For instance, you may have formed the habit of holding a cigarette a certain way, of walking or standing in a manner peculiar to you alone, or possibly of holding your head at a certain angle while talking.

Second: You must know your cover story thoroughly; know the character or characters you will have to be, inside and out, their clothes, facial expressions, gait, gestures, personal habits, thoughts and reactions. All of these things must be carefully considered and practiced ahead of time.

Keep in mind the expression, "If you tell a lie often enough you believe it yourself." If you work on being a Dr. Jekyll or Mr. Hyde hard enough, you will become that character. The student must learn his part in the same way that an actor does, and once he has acquired his new character, he must live up to it.

Remember that the enemy is sharp, but at the same time, he is also a human being and reacts, to a certain extent, like a human being. His behavior at some time may make you think that surely he has seen through your disguise. At times his actions may appear to be a deliberate test to catch you, when they are not such at all. Dispel from your mind that every little action is necessarily significant. A good rule to follow is never use a disguise except as a last resort - but when you do, play it for all it's worth. The surest way to hide is to be one of a crowd. Look and act like the others and you will not be noticed.

Before commencing work on a specific disguise, the following points should be ascertained:

1. Nature of mission.
2. Whether known in district.
3. Length of mission.
4. Cover story.
5. Second cover story.
6. Availability for advance preparation.
7. If among friends or not.

Three types of personal disguise will be discussed:

1. Temporary
2. Semi-permanent
3. Permanent

Temporary Disguise

To make yourself taller, two or two and a half inches can be quickly added to your height by tearing or folding a newspaper to form a ramp in the heels of your shoes. If you are wearing high top shoes, even more can be added. Hoist your trousers way up and tighten the belt. This will make your legs look longer.

Pick out your most prominent features. These are the ones to disguise. Wads of cotton or paper between the teeth and the cheeks will change a thin face to a fuller one. A good swarthy or dirty skin color can be had by wetting your hands and rubbing them on an old piece of rusty iron. The fume-vent of a water heater is often a good place to find it. Soot from inside a water heater or almost any stove pipe can be used to darken the eyebrows and the hair.

The sharp point of a burned match can serve as a pencil to thicken eyebrows. Try the following effects for graying hair, mustache or eyebrows; gray ashes, both wood and paper, powdered down by rubbing them in the palm of the hand. *Other methods of disguise requiring little effort;*

1. If you have round shoulders, a strong "figure eight" cord, crossed in the back, will serve as a reminder to throw out your chest and stand up straight.

2. Try the old trick of buttoning your pants to your vest to acquire a stoop.

3. Basically, posture and gait must fit the type of man you are portraying, his age, upbringing, physical condition, degree of ambition, and his whole outlook on life.

4. Start now to observe how men of different classes of society and age sit, stand and walk.

5. Building up the inside of one shoe-heel will give a "short-leg" limp.

6. A small stone or other hard object in one sock heel will produce a convincing limp.

7. Try the "lost arm," which is best done when wearing a double-breasted coat.

If it is decided that you need a second identification card or papers, make yourself up as you expect to look and have the necessary photograph taken. Several questions, however, should first be answered. Should the photograph look like one made when you were younger? Should it be taken in a different suit? Should a slightly different style of haircut or mustache (if one is to be worn) be used?

Learn how to hide your necessary disguise materials, bearing in mind that you must have them on your person. (Articles are hidden mainly to keep them from prying landlords and curious small-town officials.) Spirit gum and skin color can easily be concealed, for example, in small glass vials inside cigarettes.

Your second identification card and your hair lace mustache can be kept in your cigarette or spectacle case. Care must be exercised, however, not to flatten the hair lace, since it is the 'dressing' or shape that makes it look real.

While many of the suggestions outlined in this volume are applicable to both men and women students, the following section is written solely for the women.

A change of hair style is one of the most simple and effective aids in changing a women's appearance. If the usual style, for instance, is a "long bob", the hair should be done up, or slicked straight back into either a knot or a roll. The position of the part should be altered or eliminated altogether. If the hair is usually worn closely set, brushing it out frizzy and adding a ribbon bow will create a different effect immediately. The advisability of taking along a switch, either to add more hair or to use as a braid, should be considered. The style chosen should be one that a woman can arrange herself, naturally, without recourse to a beauty parlor. An important point to remember is that the most unbecoming hair style will probably change the wearer's appearance more than any other.

A woman of between thirty and forty years of age can easily add ten to fifteen years to her apparent age after a little instruction. She should clean off all make-up, wrinkle up her face, and with a very sharp Factor's brown eyebrow pencil lightly line all of the creases. Rub these down to the point where they are only soft shadows.

Semi-Permanent Disguise

The following deals with prepared items needed to cover a period of short operation in the field, and also with aids which you can use in the field for special jobs, particularly at night.

Semi-permanent disguise requires more time to apply than temporary disguise, and many of the items can be used only with the help of someone who has received instruction in make-up. There are, however, certain definite lines upon which to work.

Skin Color

One of the great drawbacks of make-up has always been that when ordinary skin colors are used, whether grease paint or pancake, they usually look like make-up. The color range is also limited. The formulas have been worked out on the theory that the make-up must come off easily. For our requirements just the reverse is necessary. It must look completely natural even upon close inspection, the range of colors must be unlimited, and the material must stand under different conditions without needing constant care and touching up.

With these requirements in mind, special experiments were conducted in the cosmetic research laboratories of Max Factor in Hollywood, where their chief chemists, their formulas and the benefit of their years of experience in cosmetology were made available for this purpose. Day after day formulas were tried and tested for range of color, ease of application, effect on the skin and staining qualities. Primarily a semi-permanent chemical skin stain was sought, with the Far East in mind. The object was to find something that anyone could put on smoothly, that would look real and that would last for a period of days under every anticipated condition. A few stains approached the requirements but each had some particular fault. These limitations applied also to available walnut stains.

In using skin color, the eyes and the hair should blend with it. Usually the eyes should be carefully shadowed. Most olive-skinned people, for example, have a slightly darker pigmentation on both upper and lower lids.

The following color and application may be used to receive the necessary effects;

Good for Greek or Latin

4 GL
$^3/_4$ grams, Red 21, 2.25 c.c., Good Latin color applied.
$^{13}/_4$ grams, 8L Yellow, 5.6 c.c., Thin, get grease off face.
1 gram, Ivo-black, 1.9 c.c., first; darken eyebrows and hair.
For the Far East

4 FE
$^3/_4$ gram, Red 21, 1.5 c.c., Dark brown, blackish.
1 gram, 8L Yellow, 3.2 c.c., Hindu
$^{11}/_2$ gram, Ivo-black, 2.85 c.c.
And so on.

Eyes that appear close together (less than the width of one eye apart) can be "separated" by carefully plucking the brows to widen the distance between them so that they begin no closer than a line directly above each tear-duct. They can even start a little further out than that. The reverse is applicable for "separating" the eyes.

The student who has a set of dental plates or removable bridges that show has a distinct advantage over those who do not. The sinking in of the mouth which results when the plates are removed means that half the battle toward looking older has been won. Try discoloring ordinary teeth around the gum line with iodine. A gold cap for a front tooth catches the eye and has been used effectively more than once. It can be either taken off or put on in a split second.

Let your hair grow out when you are going into a poor area or expect to assume one of certain types of covers should be thought of well ahead of time. Shampooing-out all the grease will often lighten the color of your hair two or three shades. Dyeing a student's hair to change his/her appearance before he enters an enemy area has been successful many times. Before you have your hair dyed, an allergy test must be made.

Contact lenses are the only alternative for a student who would otherwise have to wear thick noticeable lenses. While they have many advantages, their drawbacks should be pointed out. Scars, minor wounds, abrasions, burns, tropical ulcers and sores that look real can all be simulated by someone who has learned how to handle the necessary materials. Personal instruction, however, based on experience, is required.

Permanent Disguise

Permanent disguise requires the services of a plastic surgeon. It is mentioned in order that attention may be called to some of the changes that have been accomplished by facial surgery. Its use has been successfully employed in individual cases where a valuable agent who had a particularly noticeable feature, such as a prominent nose, ears that stick far out, or an easily remembered scar, might have been recognized on returning to the field.

Surgery has been used to alter the racial characteristics of Jewish students before they entered the field. Broken, bulbous and sharp Roman noses have also been successfully changed to shapes less eye-catching. Nose operations usually require about a week to ten days' hospital care, but a month must be counted upon before all swelling has gone down and the resulting "black eyes" have disappeared. One advantage is that there are no outside scars.

Prominent ears are dealt with by pinning them back. This leaves a small inconspicuous scar where the skin joins the ear to the head. Two to three weeks should be allowed for this procedure to heal.

Scars that show are definite and dangerous marks of identification which should always be eliminated if possible. They can be removed surgically by a specialist without requiring hospitalization. An operation lasting two to three hours and removal of stitches after seven to ten days are all that are necessary.

Tattoo marks are extremely difficult to remove and very dangerous for your mission. The process for removal is long and painful and not recommended. A more satisfactory treatment is re-tattooing with a larger and more elaborate design which would perhaps fit the background geography for your mission. Skillful blending can achieve very satisfactory results. It has the advantage of speed and there is much less discomfort to the subject.

* * *

Bill Brooker would then thank his students for being so patient and admonish them to remember their lesson and have a safe and successful mission.

Each recruit was assigned a project, a realistic facsimile of his or her ultimate mission. All the agent's time was taken up in acquiring and rehearsing the necessary skills and information for the project's success. "Schemes", or field training exercises, were mounted whenever possible and were designed to stress observation, shadowing and evading surveillance, physical self-defence, weapons training, sabotage, use of secret codes and ciphers, and interrogation of prisoners. When required, specialized courses were given in such things as underwater demolition and the handling of two-man submarines.

In order to make these "schemes" as realistic as possible, agents were sent out into the field as often as practical. Parachute drops into wooded areas were practiced in the Orono Forest, near Rice Lake, some made from less than one thousand feet. The General Motors plant in Oshawa and DIL's facilities in Ajax were penetrated and tagged by agents acting out their roles as saboteurs.

On occasion, the agents' success in penetrating "secure" installations caused some embarrassment to the authorities. A Yugoslav, who spoke only a few words of English, was deposited on the Queen Street street car near Spadina Avenue in Toronto. After asking for directions from a neighbouring barber shop, he successfully penetrated the naval yards and walked out with some highly secret communications manuals.

Secrecy and discretion were, needless to say, of the utmost importance as "loose lips sink ships." To illustrate just how important, one day one of the men was granted a leave and decided to go home to Sudbury, Ontario, for the weekend. On Saturday night he went out to a local bar with a few friends. They had a great time. Upon his return on Monday, Brooker called a meeting of the Camp personnel where this individual was astonished to hear Brooker read out almost word for word everything that the man had said to his friends that previous Saturday night. It goes without saying that it did not happen again and that it served as a good lesson for the others.

Any time that a day pass was given out by the Commandant to one of the staff at the Camp, a call would go out simultaneously to Inspector George McClellan of the RCMP. An RCMP agent would be assigned to follow the individual regardless of where the staff member was headed and the tail would remain with this person until he returned to the Camp.

U. R. Requested

2 REFRAIN
FROM CARELESS
TALK

BRITISH SECURITY CO-ORDINATION

46. It was not unusual for an individual on a day pass from the Camp to find a card such as this mysteriously appear befor him, an indication that he was being observed and warned.

Mac McDonald recalls one evening when he had a pass to go to Oshawa. Sergeant Paterson was with him and they decided to go to the Genosha Hotel. Upon entering the lobby, Mac told Paterson that he wanted to use the phone to see if a friend of his was at home. As he entered the phone booth, Mac noticed a man standing in a nearby corner, smoking a cigarette. When Mac hung up the phone and stepped out of the booth, he asked the man for a light. Mac said to the man, "What are you doing way out here?"

The man replied, "Oh, just visiting some friends."

Mac said, "Well, I guess I'll be seeing you around." He walked into the hotel with Sergeant Paterson.

Mac realized of course that this was an RCMP tail. He knew he could expect to see the man for the rest of the evening.

* * *

"Throughout all the training at the Camp, the emphasis was on realism and, as a result, only live ammunition was used. These exercises as observed by Colonel Smith of Oshawa were described by him as the 'most realistic and blood-curdling exercises that I have ever seen outside a theatre of war'." Fatalities at the Camp were remarkably few, though there were a number of casualties. One prominent South American killed through a training error posed a problem to the Camp authorities. Burial at the Union Cemetery in Oshawa was out of the question since identification of a neutral in a country that was at war would be a serious breach of security. Likewise, some explanation would subsequently be required when this South American was missed in his native land. A solution was reached by deciding to return the remains to their country of origin. To preserve security, the body was sewn into a diplomatic bag and sent the normal courier route to New York and then back to South America.

47. Major Fairbairn illustrates the art of silent killing. Within a moment of shaking hands with Fairbairn, the unsuspecting man can only muster up a silent gasp before death.

"One recruit who survived both the training and his subsequent mission described his commando instruction as the 'most bloody minded thing I'd ever seen.' The N.C.O. in charge always wore his kilt no matter what the exercise or the weather and nearly killed us with his crazy schemes...We had to be 'on' night and day...They never let up trying to catch us out on some detail. I don't know how often we blew up (in simulation) trains with (mock) plastique on the Toronto-Montreal line. After a few times, the poor engineers would spot us lying in the long grass by the tracks and throw up their hands. I guess they thought we were local patriots getting ready for the invasion, or subversive nuts...It paid off though...I got through my mission and managed to avoid the concentration camps."

Detailed accounts of the missions undertaken by well-trained and highly successful graduates of Camp X are only slowly and sporadically coming to light. Some are now part of the public domain, but the stories of many will probably never by known. Most of the operatives trained at Camp X prefer anonomity, and, for them, silence has been the rule and the law for most of the past sixty years. From those bits and pieces of their stories which have been disclosed, it is abundantly clear that these operatives were singularly dedicated, exhibited bravery far and above the call of duty, and that many, too many, never returned from their missions.

The Camp was much more than just a base for the training of agents. The facility was also used by the BSC as a proving ground and as a research facility for the diverse requirements of espionage activity.

Throughout the entire secret war, it was essential that all aspects of the different departments be kept in total secrecy, even from each other. It was imperative, for example, that an MI6 mission going on in the Balkans not be known about by the officers in charge of an MI6 mission going on in France. The reason, of course, was that, were an agent to be captured, he would not have any knowledge of other operations and, even under the worst type of torture, could not divulge any information about them.

With the establishment of the SOE, it was evident early on in the war that there were not enough ethnic communities in Great Britain to provide the number of partisan agents required for the corresponding countries in mainland Europe. The targeted area for recruits quickly expanded to include Canada because of the larger number of such communities, many with populations in excess of fifteen thousand. From the outset, the Canadians recruited and trained at Camp X and destined for SOE, would be part of the group called "Special Forces", an organization made up of three branches.

The first branch dealt with sabotage. The second served as liaison with the resistance and also trained the local ethnic groups accordingly. The third branch was responsible for finding safe routes back to Britain for Allied pilots who had been shot down, captured and held prisoner behind enemy lines, and for returning them as quickly as possible to the war effort.

It is also important to point out that, of the assembly line of agents trained at Camp X who would then go on to Britain to complete their training, only fifty percent would actually go on to missions behind enemy lines. The training provided at Camp X was merely preliminary in order to determine who was up to the task physically, mentally and psychologically. Those who did not meet the rigid qualifications were culled out before they were sent on to finish their training. Finally, immediately prior to departure on his mission, the agent was given a final opportunity to decline. A number of agents did just that. This fine tuning by the SOE officers at that stage insured that only top-of-the-line agents who were totally prepared for their missions would carry on and afford the SOE the best opportunity for the success of that particular mission.

The Canadians who were recruited locally and trained at Camp X comprised the highest percentage of those who did indeed go on to their missions behind enemy lines. The agent had to excel in unarmed combat and the use of small arms, and he also had to qualify as a parachute jumper. He would train extensively with the use of a compass and map in a remote and unknown area miles from the Camp. His objective, of course, was to return quickly and safely to Camp, much as he would have to reach a specific destination after having been "dropped" in the region where his mission would ultimately take place.

If the agent decided at the final briefing for his mission that he was not able to complete it, he was taken out of the assignment and sent off to a Camp in the Scottish Highlands where he would spend the remainder of the War. It is ironic that of the various groups of trainees that went through Camp X and the subsequent finishing school training, the Canadians had the largest percentage of drop-outs that did not make it to their final mission, but yet of those who did go on to do so, they had the most successful end result in each of their respective endeavors.

The finished agent was finely tuned and prepared for any eventuality. He had to be able to "think on his feet" and, were he to be stopped and interrogated, he also had to be able to formulate reasonable and acceptable responses. In the event that he had to escape or to abort a mission, he had to sense whom he could trust to help him and know how to remain inconspicuous within the local population. Finally, in the worst case, he had to know how to conduct himself if captured by the Gestapo.

It has been the consensus of many historians that the superior efforts of the expert training and support staffs of Camp X may have reduced the duration of the war by six months to a year and perhaps saved hundreds of thousands of lives. Immediately prior to D-Day, for example, when it became obvious to the Germans that the invasion was to take place in Normandy and not Calais as previously supposed, they began to move their troops from Calais to Normandy for re-enforcement. They discovered all the way along, however, that saboteurs, comprised primarily of French Canadians, had been hard at work and had blown up bridges and railway lines delaying the progress of the German Army by approximately three weeks. By the time they were able to complete the repairs and eventually reach Normandy, it was too late.

The agents were trained in all types of espionage work. Camp X was indeed a school in every respect. The day began with two hours of gymnastics after breakfast each morning followed by two hours of black board theory conducted in the Lecture Hall. Then lunch, followed by another two hours of training, this time with explosives in the open fields of the Camp, then one hour of small arms practice in the basement firing range, one hour of parachute jumping from the ninety foot high jump stand which had been specially designed for Camp X, an hour of some type of sport such as football, then dinner.

48. Explosives training

After dinner it was study time, or "home work", which of course would be reviewed at the next day's lecture. This typical day would be repeated for a period of approximately six to ten weeks.

The agents had to endure rigorously structured training, perhaps an annoyance at the time, but which would prove to be invaluable to the agents once on their missions. They were forced to stand behind a bulletproof glass wall while the trainers fired live rounds of ammunition at them from a Tommy gun, and would be ordered to crawl through trenches covered with barbed wire while once again being fired upon with live rounds of ammunition.

After scouring all of the Ontario mining camps and factories across Ontario looking for secret agent material, Eric Curwain, a.k.a. Bill Simpson, was asked to go to Europe in order to continue his search and specifically look for Yugoslav men who were badly needed for action behind enemy lines. Curwain was slated to become Tito's personal radio operator but, in the process of establishing that position, something happened and Tito changed his mind. Curwain was never given an explanation. While in Italy awaiting his next orders, he spent his time interrogating German prisoners for the SIS. Once he received his orders, he departed for Hungary to work for the Russians in Russian occupied territory.

After V.E. Day, Curwain returned to Canada and his waiting wife, Vilma. When they had met for the first time, he had, of course, introduced himself as "Bill Simpson." He learned shortly after they met that Vilma had served in Intelligence as a code-breaker at Bletchly Park after the outbreak of the War, giving them a certain commonality. As their relationship grew, Vilma dreamed of becoming "Mrs. Bill Simpson," but quickly learned to forgive Bill his alias.

* * *

(Author's Note: Although much of the material relating to the subject of training 'Secret Agents' during World War II is still largely classified, I have been able to acquire some information from the FCO (Foreign and Commonwealth Office) relative to STS-103 (Camp X).

The following data was recently released to me including reports regarding the number of personnel and the different departments that trained at Camp X between January 1942, and March 1, 1943. It is estimated that between March 1, 1943 and April 30, 1944 another one hundred agents were trained for various intelligence departments.

Details of Students Trained at STS 103:

Special Operations Officers	21
Special Operations Field	58
(including 22 Yugoslavs & 3 Italians	
Special Intelligence Staff	15
Special Intelligence Field	13
OSS Officers	8
OSS Field	18
OSS Instructors	14
FBI	10
RCMP	4
British Passport Control	1
W/T Operators	19
OWI	27
Security Officers for South America	53
Psychological Warfare - West Africa	6
Psychological Warfare - U.S. Army	6
Total	*273*

Chapter IV

The Hams

Author's Note: In 1978, Eric Curwain (a.k.a. Bill Simpson) gave me an exclusive interview which was unlike any other. He talked about how he had recruited the Ham operators who would become the backbone of Hydra, the W/T (Wireless / Telegraph) operators, and agents abroad.

Again, I would like to call upon Eric's own words as he described the process in his autobiography, Almost Top Secret.)

"Among the fraternity of radio Hams in Ontario there was little difficulty in finding recruits to man the communications network planned for the Western hemisphere; that is, for countries other than the United States. Communication between Britain's SIS headquarters in England and their office in New York was provided by a radio link with the Federal Bureau of Investigation which, thanks to the efforts of William Stephenson, had become a stout comrade in arms for Britain. Our Buckhamshire radio H.Q. in England kept up a daily contact with New York. It must be admitted that the American operators were quicker with their Bug Keys than the British with their 'up and down' keys, the naval style we could not discard.

"Armed with permission from the Royal Canadian Mounted Police, I contacted the Department of Transport Inspector in charge of radio regulations for Ontario and asked him the names of the best Hams. Among the first mentioned was that of Fred Saxon, then employed in the City Hall. He was the ideal man for us; a first-class Morse operator, DX enthusiast (expert in maintaining radio contacts around the world), cheery and positive in outlook and a good disciplinarian. We at once named him Wire Chief of the newly erected radio and land line installation at Camp X located near Oshawa.

49. Fred Saxon (centre) chief radio operator, 1941

"Under the direction of Bill Stephenson's electronics expert, Colonel Benjamin De Forrest (Pat) Bayly, Fred Saxon our chief radio operator, and his constantly expanding group of operators, soon had radio and teletype linking us with the rest of the world, including London, New York and Washington.

"The operation was a triumph for Pat Bayly. To take a casual band of amateur radio operators and mold them, within a few weeks, into a loyal, hard-working team to the point where they could link up with the best professional communications networks of the United States and Britain was indeed a feat. Our links with New York and Washington were by teletype and the clatter of these machines was the background music of our Ops Room at Camp X.

"Professor Bayly's big achievement during the war was his adaptation of Western Union's Telekrypton cipher machines for the transmission of millions of code groups daily. Recalling the laborious hours of encoding and decoding messages in Warsaw using transposition tables, one realized that the 1939 era of coding was archaic and unsafe. By the outbreak of war, we had not progressed very far from the simple coding practices of World War I.

"Some aspects of American and British coding problems were revealed to me on the flight from London to Stockholm during the winter of 1939, when I met a Pathe news cameraman on his way to film the attack by Russian planes on the practically undefended city of Helsinki. He told me of a coding incident which happened after World War I at the time of the Treaty of Versailles negotiations when the American representative there had to send all his messages from Paris to Washington via the British cable system through London, the only trans-Atlantic cable available. The British Intelligence officer in Whitehall, whose job it was to hold up these American messages and decode them before they were transmitted on to Washington, was surprised one day to find at the end of a long message to President Wilson the following plea addressed to himself from the American encoding officer in Paris;

"BILL PLEASE HURRY UP DECODING OF THIS AND
SHOOT IT ON TO WASHINGTON SOON AS POSSIBLE"

"All's fair in war and peace but it must have annoyed the officials of the State Department in Washington to know that Whitehall read these vital messages before they did.

"Anyone who doubts the above story should read that most fascinating book, *The American Black Chamber,* by H.O. Yardley, brilliant head of the Cryptographic Bureau of the United States from 1913 to 1929; his book was published in 1931. The ingenuity of the American cryptographers in breaking the most complicated foreign codes, of which the Japanese electronically scrambled were the most baffling, should have warned both the British and German military and diplomatic services of World War II that none of their current codes could be considered unbreakable. Yet we now know from official records that the Germans were decoding British Naval traffic through most of World War II and the British were just as successful in breaking the German and Italian codes. The American decoding of the Japanese diplomatic and military messages has been the subject of an engrossing post-war book.

"Up to 1928, Yardley's men were still deciphering vital messages passing between foreign powers, but the then U.S. Secretary of State decided in 1929 that it was ungentlemanly to probe into the secret communications of other countries so he disbanded Yardley's office. The book by this cryptographer - retired at the age of 40 - is better than any spy story of World War I and its post-war period.

"The interviewing of our radio operators during the recruiting campaign was a pleasant duty. Each man was asked the orthodox questions, including his views about the war, and the final one - " Have you ever been in prison?"

A warning was added that if such was the case, the RCMP would disclose the fact to us. Only one admitted, after first denying it, that he had been in jail. Unfortunately we took him on, after discussions with head office, but he was the only unsuitable recruit and was eventually discharged as a trouble maker.

"The next thing was to select operators willing to serve our organization in Central and South America. The dozen or so eventually nominated for these appointments did excellent work. In age they varied from twenty to thirty years."

(Author's Note: H. Montgomery Hyde would write after the war ended, "SPIES-SABOTEURS-TRAITORS, an army of them infested the Americas, threatening Britain's lifeline to the United States, sometimes penetrating high levels of the U.S. Government."

"Bill Stephenson organized his counter-attack from his deceptively innocuous New York office, sending the men and women of Intrepid into a secret, deadly battle that reached through the hemisphere and beyond, striking at the heart of the Nazi war machine. Their weapons were espionage, daring sleight-of-hand, deception, fraud and forgery, seduction and, on occasion, more extreme methods.")

"Nearly all of our Hams were recruited in Ontario, mainly in Toronto, Hamilton and St. Catherines. Their civil occupations included postman, draughtsman, engraver, printer, technician, office worker and others. They were nearly all camera enthusiasts; many were non-smokers because they preferred to use their spare cash for buying radio supplies.

"The impressive antenna system at Camp X remained a wartime mystery to the inhabitants of the nearby communities. The camp itself was strongly guarded because not only did it house important SIS communications equipment, but was also the site of a British SOE Commando - Sabotage training centre, both units under the ultimate control of Bill Stephenson from his New York headquarters.

"The commanding officer of Camp X was an Englishman, a 'Colonel M.' From our first meeting our auras clashed. We were lunching in the mess when he broke into a violent denunciation of the Canadian Ham operators;

" 'They refuse to accept camp discipline. I won't tolerate it.'

"The majors and junior officers at the table seemed to tremble. Colonel M was a civilian by profession who had never been under fire but in some ways he outdid Colonel Blimp himself. It was useless to point out that these young Canadians were still civilians, free in their own country and, most important, expert in what Stephenson and Bayly wanted. I ventured to suggest that it would be unreasonable to downgrade them into pseudo soldiers just to improve the appearance of the local parade ground. As far as M knew, I was a civilian and beyond any "pulling of rank" approach by him.

"My phrasing was undiplomatic and from there on M refused to have any dealings with me. Our operators continued working like beavers at their radio duties and in their spare time watched the SOE and American OSS trainees practicing judo and learning the use of explosives. Some of our operators who were due to go south to Latin America took unarmed combat lessons from the Camp's instructors.

"The Judo instructor, Captain Fairbairn, well know to many Commando men in Britain, looked like a professor and was well over six feet tall. His huge right hand would grip that of the nervous beginner, assuring him with;

" 'No matter how big your adversary, if you know unarmed combat you will be able to take care of yourself.'

"He warned that a man wielding a knife could be more dangerous than one with a pistol and demonstrated this by launching himself from his bed and coming up under the pistol-bearing arm of an opponent with amazing speed.

"Judo, an extension of ju-jutsu, was used by the ancient Lama Chinese monks to protect themselves from robbers. The Japanese adopted it, adding some 300 additional holds and throws. The armed forces of several nations trained men in judo. No other sport calls for such strenuous training and study, and a knowledge of anatomy is a basic requirement. That rare judo expert who gets to the top of the nine degrees of the Black Belt category is unique in courage and stamina."

* * *

Eric Adams, another Camp X "Ham" recruit, has, in his collection of family papers, a document from the Government of Canada sent to him at the start of the war. Dated September 5, 1939, the letter was sent to him because he was a licensed radio amateur, operating in Ontario under the call sign VE3ALG.

50. Eric Adams at the Camp X re-union in 1979

The document states that, in the opinion of the government, "It is expedient that His Majesty's Government in Canada shall have control over the transmission of messages by radio stations of all classes." It states further, "I hereby notify you that your amateur experimental station license is suspended forthwith, and direct you to completely dismantle and render inoperative all equipment installed in your station."

Such were the communication capabilities of private radio transmitting and receiving equipment of even the most modest sort. Radio communication in wartime could lead to defeat or victory, triumph or disaster. This fact brought about the BSC recruitment, and the training at Camp X, of a number of Canadian amateur radio operators to assist in the interception of the incredible volume of enemy clandestine radio activity that was to spring up in all parts of the world, and which would play a major role in shaping the war.

Eric Adams was one of these BSC radio monitors, and, in his case, spent most of his war years in South America. Simply stated, an amateur radio operator was an ideal candidate for handling clandestine radio activity of any description, be it interception or the actual transmitting of traffic. The radio amateur liked and understood his hobby, he was good at solving technical problems and keeping equipment running without seeking outside assistance. He was already capable of sending and receiving Morse code efficiently and needed only to be trained in the specialties of handling clandestine radio messages.

51. Suitcase radio used for instructional purposes at Camp X

This training took Eric two or three months to complete at Camp X as a member of the first wireless class, in 1942. Later the same year, Eric was on his way to Caracas, Venezuela, where he was posted at what was then the British Legation (later an Embassy), supposedly as a cipher clerk. He then had a stint under cover at the British controlled oil fields, at a place called El Meme, in a tiny community in the jungle near Maracaibo.

(Author's Note: Eric came to Camp X through the same recruitment methods as his friend, Bill Hardcastle. In fact, they arrived at Camp X on the same day, in the same army truck. Both men were targeted for South America but, as it turned out, Bill was deemed to be invaluable to Hydra and Eric was best suited for the mission in South America. Thus, both men said their good byes and went their separate ways.)

While in Venezuela, Eric was one of a team of two BSC monitors. His colleague was another Toronto radio amateur who later went on to Trinidad while Eric went much farther south to Santiago, Chile, where he remained until the end of the war. Other Canadian radio amateurs from Camp X who took part in this South American venture were stationed at Bogota, Colombia; Quito, Ecuador; Lima, Peru; Buenos Aires, Argentina and Montevideo, Uruguay.

The importance of clandestine radio communication to the enemy war effort can be simply explained. There is probably no more perishable commodity than the information gathered by spies. As the war progressed, it was commonly taking a month or more for various secret couriers and methods to relay information from enemy, or neutral, territory to Germany. With radio, the actual transmission took only seconds or, at the most, minutes.

The significance of South America was due in part to the facts that the nationals maintained a different attitude toward the war, and that there were fewer heavily-populated areas. These and other factors made it easier to maintain illicit radio stations with less chance of detection or interference from authorities. There is also the consideration that radio signals tend to travel better north-to-south then east-to-west across the Atlantic. Smaller, low-output (more easily hidden and harder to locate), illicit transmitters in the U.S. were used to send data regarding ship movements and other vital information to South America for relaying, by means of more powerful transmitters, to Germany.

In the clandestine radio 'business', there is an 'out station' which is secretly located in enemy or neutral territory. There is also the main station back home which is called the 'control' or 'home station.'

Hamburg, or more accurately Wohldorf, just outside the city limits, was the control point for a vast volume of German clandestine traffic. Working from underground bunkers, this activity went on unabated, even during the time that Hamburg was being turned into rubble by daily and nightly Allied air attacks. Eric used to listen with amazement, night after night, to clandestine radio circuits working back to Hamburg, at a time when the city was little more than a blazing ruin.

In fact, one of Eric's main priorities was monitoring a circuit which, in the BSC parlance, was identified as 13/43, a number which would remain in his memory for the rest of his life. The designation "13" meant Hamburg and indicated the location of the control station, while "43" meant that this was the forty third circuit that had been identified with Hamburg as its home station.

Also engraved in Eric's mind was the signal "BJ". This was a code used by 13/43 and it meant a change of frequency to ten thousand, four hundred kilocycles. Eric had been supplied with a whole list of these frequency-change signals (although there was a tendency to use only a couple of them), and he knew exactly what was meant by these cryptic two letter signals, usually used when reception was poor at one end or the other.

For many years afterward, Eric still thought of 5:30 p.m. as the time 13/43 came on the air, sometimes as often as seven times a week. It was one of the most professional operations which he monitored. With the out-station in Argentina, contact with Hamburg would sometimes be made within a second or two and the traffic started instantly. You had to be on your toes.

Oddly enough, if the reception was first class, Eric was not very happy. This almost always meant that the Hamburg operator would have difficulty as a result of weakened signals and since 13/43 did not do much frequency adjustment, the transmission instead would be abruptly halted. The German operator might first try a change of frequency but often, if that did not rectify the signal, would throw in a time lapse as well, perhaps going off the air for two hours and coming back on later on a different frequency.

Clandestine radio traffic was almost always in five-letter cipher groups. Only in rare instances was anything else used, although in one of the most dramatic moments of Eric's wartime activity, at something like 3:00 a.m., a station he was monitoring came up with the incredible message in plain English, "I have lost my code book".

Eric had no idea of the significance of this circuit, beyond the fact that he had been told that it was of the highest importance. It was operating on a low frequency and signal strength was good, suggesting that it was a communication from a relatively nearby point and intended to be received at close range. Perhaps it might be an agent in Chile or Argentina signaling a submarine off shore.

The use of plain English ('en-clair', as non-coded messages are called) deserves explanation. Operators of German clandestine stations were taught an assortment of English phrases and words for occasional or special use. Presumably the idea was to give a casual interceptor the idea that he was listening to an American or British service and thus move on. It was a futile, almost silly, device because the sending style and other operating techniques of a clandestine station were such that they were readily recognizable long before they transmitted more than a couple of words in English.

Although monitoring activities spanned, theoretically, a twenty four hour day and there was no other BSC operator in Santiago, Eric still had free time to acquaint himself with a totally foreign world. During the war, travel to South America from North America was limited largely to people related to the war effort. Flight down was on a DC3, a slow flying aircraft that left at daybreak and flew until dusk, stopping only to refuel.

A flight from the top of South America to Santiago involved three days' travel. There was no after dark flying and there were times when planes were grounded by the weather for days. Once flights over the Andes to Argentina were held up for a couple of weeks. On Eric's flight down, he had the unique experience of having a German agent as his seat partner, a fact which he did not discover until later. When Eric got off at Santiago, the German continued to Buenos Aires where he was arrested. All this information reached Eric through his BSC station boss. Eric had a few anxious moments, trying desperately to recall whether or not he had said anything indiscreet, although his recollection was that the German had shown no more than a casual interest to his seat mate and had asked no questions of significance.

Once, in the middle of the night, Eric awoke in the bedroom of his Santiago boarding house to realize that the door was creeping slowly open and someone was obviously on the other side. For a person in Eric's line of work, it was an alarming moment and, taking into account his doubtful skills at unarmed combat during his brief training at Camp X, he decided it would be best to get out of bed and at least die standing up.

52. Camp X from the air looking West

Eric leapt out on the far side and switched on the light. There, in the half open door, profusely apologizing, stood a young man in the gray uniform of a private in the Chilean army. He had been upstairs "visiting" the maid, and, in attempting to find his way back to the street in the darkened household, he had become confused and had opened the wrong door.

A much more serious incident took place during Eric's brief stay in

Venezuela. Eric and a colleague who were on their way from the British Legation to where they were living in the suburbs, became aware of a man who seemed very interested in them. At the bus station, he stood watching just a few yards away. Buses came and went but the man never boarded any of them. Finally, the suburban bus which Eric and his colleague normally would have taken pulled in and, to test their suspicions, they ignored it until it was pulling away. At the latest possible moment, they raced to the open back door and leapt aboard. Their pursuer did the same thing at the open front door.

They lived virtually at the end of the bus line and, as they neared their destination, the two men and their suspicious companion were the only remaining passengers. It was like a scene from a Hitchcock movie.

They tried their ploy in reverse. As the bus reached their stop and paused, no one moved. Then as it picked up speed they jumped off the back, raced across the road and down their dark street. They heard running footsteps behind them, but the footsteps had not yet reached the entrance to their street. In the several seconds remaining, Eric and his friend dodged behind some large bushes. The footsteps ran by and faded away, and the two men crossed the street to where they lived and went quickly but safely inside.

The next morning, Eric's BSC station chief listened with interest and eventually showed him a series of police mug shots. Eric identified his "traveling companion." He was well-known and dangerous.

The conclusion was that it was probably a case of mistaken identity on the part of the pursuer. There had been recent activity in which jewelry, intended to be smuggled to Spain to help finance the Axis war effort, had been intercepted and confiscated because of a BSC tip-off to local authorities. It was felt that the follower may have believed that Eric had been involved and was out to even things up.

Not all of Eric's activities took on such an exciting "James Bond" touch. Some were humble and far more mundane. In Santiago, as the only electronics personnel on the premises, Eric was viewed as a sort of repairman for the hearing aid used by the wife of the British ambassador. She was a charming and delightful woman, but obligated to carry around a hearing aid, which in those days was a cumbersome box several times bigger than today's portable radios and which, from time to time, had things go wrong with it.

Eric very much liked South America. He was saddened at the vicious inflation and the military dictatorships that were so prevalent. When he was in Chile, the unit of currency was the peso, worth about three cents in Canadian currency. Fifteen pesos bought a very good bottle of wine for which Chile is famous. It was even possible to buy a bottle of cheap wine for only three pesos. There was a twenty-centavo coin (one peso has one hundred centavos) which would pay for a street car fare.

The people of Chile, were intensely democratic and law-abiding. Day or night, Eric went without fear to almost any part of the city. He was never involved in or even witness to any sort of violence. Once, on a Chilean street-car, Eric was amazed to hear (in startling contrast to the Toronto of the 1940's from which he had come) its poorly dressed conductor berating a drunken passenger and telling him that he should be ashamed, that his conduct was dishonourable.

The attitude of Chileans toward the war varied. Some were distinctly pro-German, others pro-Allied and many were somewhat neutral. On balance, in Chile, the population favoured the Allies. Some movie theatres showed the normal featured pictures, but others, called "rotativos", specialized in running continuous showings of news reels. The audiences commonly applauded when Roosevelt or Churchill appeared on the screen.

It must be understood, of course, that knowledge of German death camps and the mass murders of millions were not public knowledge at this time. Later on, toward the end of the war, when pictures of these places were first released, there was general public revulsion.

An indication of the somewhat ambivalent attitude of the Chileans is illustrated by an episode that happened to Eric in a bar. He was approached by a man who asked if Eric was American or English, the term "Canadian" was bewildering to many Latin Americans. He eventually presented to Eric, for several pesos, a cut-out of Churchill doing obscene things to a Hitler cut-out. Eric was quite sure that had he indicated German sympathies, he would have been presented with a the same cut-out but with the "partici-pants" reversed.

Chapter V

Hydra

(Author's note: The code name 'Hydra' was given to the wireless installation because it was like the "mythical beast of the same name, a 'many headed', triple diversity creature" which would communicate continuously during the war years with England.)

When Bill Hardcastle (Yorkie) had his first interview with Bill Simpson, he had no idea that he was going to be trained as a secret agent! He believed that he indeed was going to be doing something top secret having to do with Morse Code, but it was only at his second interview, this time with Tommy Drew-Brook, that he found out that the BSC had plans for him in South America.

Bill was intrigued by the possibility and was very much looking forward to his new assignment. After all, he had gone from his mundane job at The Toronto Star to becoming an agent-in-training all in just a few days.

At the time that Bill was being trained, the Camp was determined to be an excellent location for the transfer of code, much better than was Ottawa. The topography of the land and the lake made it an excellent site and signals would arrive distinctly and rapidly from the UK. Because there was a shortage of expert radio operators, Bill soon realized that any hope of his being posted as a secret agent overseas was dwindling rapidly. There was a much greater need for trained personnel to build and operate Hydra.

As mentioned previously, the building that would house Hydra was the most mysterious looking building at the Camp. It was a four-sided structure, completely open on the inside, with windows all around but placed seven feet above the ground for obvious reasons of secrecy. The building had only one entrance and that was at the front; two large doors making it easy to bring in large equipment.

53. The radio room—note the headsets at right

One day, not long after Bill arrived, a large van drove into the Camp and delivered crates of communications components. When it all was unloaded, someone yelled, "Go to it, fellows!" Bill and his mates proceeded to build a complete, working communications installation from a photograph. They hooked it up, and Hydra was born!

Bill has often been asked where they were able to find the parts for the Hydra operation. There was a lot of money available to them, so Bayly and his men simply went around buying entire sets from amateurs here and in the U.S. The Camp acquired a "1-KW (one thousand watts) rig from Toronto with monstrous tubes but very well designed." It, too, arrived at the Camp in pieces to be re-assembled on site.

*54. Hydra arrived as components from various sources-
here it sits in its containers, ready for assembly*

Most of the big transmitter complex was "Jerry-built." Parts came from everywhere. "One transmitter had been a 10-KW (ten thousand watts) station in Philadelphia, WCAU. It was highly experimental and years ahead of its time. Governments appropriated and shut down such rigs for obvious reasons when war broke out, as they presented a potential threat to national security, and as well, provided installations such as the Camp's, with state of the art equipment."

By the time Bill "completed his course at Camp X, he was prepared to undertake a clandestine wireless operation in South America. He was trained to intercept, decode, re-code and then transmit messages back to North America. German submarines were a likely source of radio traffic in Buenos Aires, where Bill was told he was headed. Actually Bill, and his partner Jack, from Toronto, were to cover South America as far south as Lima, Peru. Most of that continent was fairly heavily involved. Clearly Hitler's next blow was aimed there, or so it seemed in 1942. Bill was anxiously awaiting his posting since he had been told that Buenos Aires was a hot bed of German agents."

Bill and Jack were told that they were short of space at the Camp and that the two men were to stay in Toronto until contacted, so they waited for some word as to what was happening. Eventually they were advised that the plan had been aborted and that they would not be needed anymore. After Bill heard the news, he "went off and joined the Air Force (RCAF) as he had tried to do earlier, but had not been called up because of his colour-blindness." However, because it was now wartime, the Air Force overlooked the colour-blindness as they were short of wireless operators. The very day that Bill Hardcastle joined the Air Force, Bill Simpson contacted him and said that he was needed right away. Naturally, Bill (Hardcastle) had to tell him that he was "too late." Simpson's response was typically brief. "Don't worry at all. I'll take care of it". So, while Bill was awaiting his instructions, he attended one course at the Air Force training centre. He received all A's and the Air Force made him an instructor.

He was assigned to Montreal, Quebec, as an instructor-in-training. "Each trainee had to start coding at one word per minute, but the instructor said that Bill, who was already capable of working much faster, would not have to sit in because it would be a waste of his time." The day that Bill was informed that he was to be an instructor, he thanked them for the offer, but indicated that he expected he would be "going back to Toronto." Sure enough, the very next day he was back at Camp X wearing an RCAF uniform. He was given permission to keep the uniform as he was entitled to wear it, which he did proudly. At the Camp, he was the only personnel in RCAF dress.

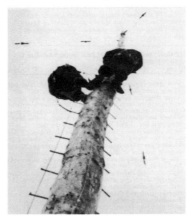

55. Ontario Hydro workers erect Rhombic Antennae for Hydra

Things were going "very well", even after Bill had gone back to the Camp, until the Air force lost record of his address. Somehow they had muddled a few numbers and Bill's pay cheques were going to "1145 King Street, in care of Hardcastle, Aircraftsman," and then ultimately to the dead letter office. They should in fact have been sent to "25 King Street, Room 1145 (BSC HQ in Toronto)." Bill went to the Air Force paymaster and was informed that they had accumulated approximately three thousand dollars in back pay for him. Innocently Bill said, "I'm sorry, I can't take it." Bill tried to refuse the pay because he felt he was not entitled to it, but the paymaster was adamant. He said he did not care what had happened but he just wanted to clear up his bookkeeping. Bill got in touch with Drew-Brook who told him to, "Just leave it there."

The Camp Commandant ordered Bill to go to British Columbia to complete a wireless course run by the Air Force. The course instructor did not realize that Bill had experience with high priority transmissions as he was unaware that Bill had previously trained at Camp X. For that matter, he was not likely even aware of the Camp's existence. One morning, he looked over the forty five students in the class and told them that a coded message consists of the preamble "P", for priority and then the type of priority, such as "OU". The OU indicated "Top Priority". Then he said, " None of you buggers will ever see anything like it, but I'll mention it anyway." Little did he know that Bill had been putting these transmissions through the Camp, almost routinely, every day.

"An OU message goes straight to the heads of state and military chiefs of staff. Such messages obviously contained information requiring the highest level of security clearance." Bill found the instructor's attitude amusing but never let it be known exactly what his own position was.

Once the equipment was operational, Bill Hardcastle and Bernie Sandbrook personally sent the very first messages from Hydra to England. Occasionally, the English sergeants would come into the radio room and plead with Bill and Bernie to be allowed a crack at sending some Morse. These sergeants had been wireless instructors in Hong Kong prior to its capture by the Japanese, and they were first rate in their work at the Camp. Once in a while Bill broke down and let them 'send' (transmit) as he did not see any harm in it. "They were very good, and the codes were indecipherable anyway."

Bill and his colleagues would receive German messages which had been intercepted by our agents in South America, re-coded, and then sent along to us. Ironically, had Bill been sent to South America as originally planned by the BSC, he would have been sending these very same messages instead of receiving them.

56. Erection of the numerous Rhombic Antennae took place over several months using poles supplied by Ontario Hydro

Hydra had direct access to Ottawa, New York, and Washington using lines belonging to Bell Telephone, as well as to Canadian National and Canadian Pacific. The use of these lines was very costly, but the "Bell representative told Bill that the Camp had a higher priority than even the Prime Minister's Office." When the Camp wanted something repaired or serviced, Bell would be there immediately!

(Author's Note: During my interviews with Bill Hardcastle, he was able to give me accurate and concise information as to how the Hydra operation was set up and how nothing would have worked without the massive rhombic antennae which were donated and erected by Ontario Hydro.)

"There were three sets of these rhombic (diamond-shaped) antennae, each set strung between four telephone poles stretching from Thornton Road to Corbett Creek. Mr. Edmonds, from Ontario Hydro, worked at the Camp and it was he who selected the poles and looked after the construction.

"The beauty of the rhombic design is in its ability to cover the greatest number of frequencies in the least amount of space. In addition, these rhombics had very high gain (sensitivity), and a slow fade-out effect. The technology was fairly new, but very sophisticated. The antennae had air, dried in silica, pumped through them into the dipole (hollow 'wire') to maintain a dielectric charge.

"The three sets of rhombics fed into one triple diversity receiver. These three fragments were blended into a single signal which was then stored as a series of raised dots on paper tapes. One of the most senior of the officers was a leading expert in short wave and rhombic theory. He would go out at night and 'shoot' the Pole (North) Star; there was no room for error." During winter ice storms, quite marvelous displays of The Northern Lights could be witnessed on the rhombics. One guard actually thought they were under attack by the enemy the first time he saw this phenomenon.

The busiest time in the radio room was during the day because radio signals can be "made to bounce or 'skip' off the electrically charged ionosphere perfectly during the day but, at night, they often produce fade-out." It would require three "skips" for the signal to go from the Camp to England. The signal bounced down from the ionosphere to the ocean's surface and back up and so on until it was received by another of the rhombics in England.

57. Inside Hydra — note the high windows

Information was stored on different types of paper tape, each a little different in size and in the spacing of the dots and dashes. In-coming messages were automatically stored as dots on tape and then re-transmitted later. In the evening, when things were quieter, they would run the tapes through a "Bomack machine which cranked the data out at 190 words per minute. Most of the time, things went along fairly routinely and Hydra functioned simply as a clearing house for information from the embassies in Washington" and other foreign centers.

One day the installation was nearly put off the air permanently due to carelessness. Someone had been using the "XMTTR" (transmitter) and went to the mess at supper time. He sat down next to Bill Hardcastle. Bill asked, "Who's at the radio?" The man answered casually that he had finished at four o'clock and did not know who, if anyone, had replaced him. That meant that the radio was "on" but that it was probably not being driven.

Bill "ran across the road and opened the doors." The heavy smoke just about knocked him down and he could see a roaring red fire in the corner. The fire extinguisher was on the opposite wall from where he stood. Bill fought his way to it through the dense black smoke and deployed the extinguisher, but its capacity was not sufficient to put the fire out. Bill "grabbed three buckets of sand that were kept nearby." He knew that the sand could potentially destroy the transmitter, but he figured that the "XMTTR" was "ruined by now anyway" so he threw bucket after bucket of the sand on it, finally smothering the flames. The fire had nearly consumed the new XMTTRs which Hughey Durrant and Bill had just finished installing.

58. Part of Hydra's main transmitter - note tuning coil on top of cabinet at right

"There was no off/on safety switch on the transmitter. If you had reason to go behind the XMTTR you took the risk of tangling with five thousand volts of electricity. Many times men came close to 'getting it' back there."

Anticipating a particularly busy day, Bill Hardcastle, Hughey Durrant and Bernie Sandbrook were once asked to work in the Communications Building on the Morse machines. Bill recalled that he was working the teletype machines. The raw data would come in through Hydra and flow through to the Communications Building where it would be printed out in five-letter code.

Bill and the others were receiving coded messages from England that particular day, turning them around and Morse Coding them to BSC in New York. Suddenly, a flurry of OU "Top Priority" messages starting flying out onto the printer, one after the other.

(Author's note: An OU message was the highest level of priority that was established. If an OU message was received, everything else ceased automatically and the OU message was processed immediately.)

Bill was so alarmed by this seemingly endless stream of about fourteen OU messages that he did exactly what he was trained to do; he dropped everything else and started pounding out the keys to New York as quickly as he could. At the same time he turned to his fellow mates and said, "Hey boys, I think this is it! I think the invasion has started!"

An excellent guess; it was June 6, 1944!

'D' Day!

Chapter VI

The Training & Missions

Andy Daniels sat silently in the hollow shell of the Halifax Bomber, oblivious to what was going on around him. The flashing red light beside the open drop chute was all he could see. The others with him were equally quiet.

He took another sip from his flask of rum while he stared at the light which constantly flashed in his face, wondering how soon would it turn green? At that moment he had no idea where he was, only that soon he would drop through that chute and into the unknown. What would be waiting for him when he reached the ground? Had the enemy been tipped off about his arrival? Would the Gestapo be waiting for him when he landed? He took another sip from his flask and stared at the flashing light...

59. A Halifax plane with its crew.

Andy thought back to the day when he had sat in the shade of a tree trying to escape a June heat wave at Camp Borden, Ontario. A corporal came running in his direction. "Private, the Commanding Officer would like to see you", the corporal said. Andy went to the CO who ordered him to report to the Canadian National Exhibition Grounds in Toronto, a staging area for soldiers about to be shipped overseas.

Once there, Andy was joined by eight other Hungarian/Canadian boys, all of whom he recognized. They were all packed into an army Jeep, then later into a civilian car, and in less than two hours, they arrived at Camp X. Of course, Andy had no idea where or what this place was. All he knew was that they were in a secluded, secret Camp.

As Andy and the others stepped into the building to which they had been directed, he immediately knew where their mission would take them. The reception room had been converted into their Hungarian "homeland" complete with food, folk art pieces, and wine.

Training started that first night - drinking good Hungarian wine! Naturally, the young recruits did not look upon this as a training exercise but more as a reception or a bit of R & R before their actual training would begin. Their trainers, however, certainly took it more seriously. This was the very purpose of the exercise: to learn to be able to drink as much as was possible and still hold your tongue. Some months later this training paid off, as will become apparent as Andy's story continues to unfold.

Training went on day and night. Daytime instruction dealt with the basic skills; then, as the trainees advanced, night time instructions were added. The training was intensive, to say the least. Every minute of the day was filled. The agents were kept either running or crawling; they seldom walked anywhere. They might be either silently crawling up to a target or stealing away from it. The same exercise was repeated over and over until it was pounded into them and became an integral part of their nervous systems, until each reaction was so automatic that it became a sixth sense.

"We had to go into a dark room in the old Sinclair farmhouse where we would find a bag of gun parts. Still in the dark, we had to put them together and come out shooting."

An obstacle course was constructed through which the agents suffered the most rigorous and grueling instruction. Specialty equipment was often received from American manufacturers, occasionally obtained with the direct intervention of President Roosevelt. Corning Glass received a request for, and subsequently provided, a sheet of bullet proof glass some six feet high and nine feet wide. Agents would stand behind this glass while live ammunition was fired directly at them from short range.

The following pictures were smuggled out of Camp X, copied and actually appeared in a local Toronto newspaper in 1943. They were then smuggled back into the Camp. The agent-in-training responsible for this 'operation' had created a cover story to protect himself. If he were to be caught, he would simply say that he was practicing what he had been taught to see how proficient he was, then he could return the pictures immediately. As it turned out, he did not get caught and he performed his self-proclaimed mission successfully. Photographs such as this of the agents' training were taken routinely and became part of Major Fairbairn's Instruction Manual.

60. A secret agent crawls across the open fields of Camp X with the instructions ingrained in his head, "To avoid detection, be still."

61. A Camp X Instructor shows an agent in training how to kill a man from behind.

62. An agent infiltrates the Camp during his simulated mission inside Camp X.

One might wonder why it was so important to the agent in the field as well as the guard responsible for guarding the Camp to both be trained in all of these procedures. Whether the agent was attempting to "infiltrate" the Camp, or the guard was trying to prevent him from doing so, it was beneficial to both to understand the actions of the other. One only need read the following quote from Andy (Durovecz) Daniels' book, *My Secret Mission,* to see why.

"I was questioned by the Gestapo as well. Once again I had to describe the methods and locations of my training, but I told them no more than I had told the Hungarians. Since I had come through Slovakia, they too tried to discover, by fair means or foul, whether I was not a "Bolshie" and a Soviet agent, giving me many a beating in the process. What they really wanted to know were the intentions of the British concerning Hungary. Where, and in which direction would the British carry out a major attack on the Balkans? How many British soldiers and airmen were being prepared for action in Hungary? I could honestly say I didn't know.

"Once, while questioning me, the Gestapo suddenly started talking about Camp X! Where was it? What kind of training took place there? They asked me much that I really did not know. We did not even know at that time about the code name, "Camp X"; the people around Whitby and Oshawa had merely called it "the secret military camp." This showed how well informed the Abwehr (the German Secret Service) were; they even knew the code name. But they did not bother me much about this, perhaps because they knew no more, perhaps because my demeanour suggested it really was news to me."

My old friend Andy was right. As indicated previously, every intelligence agency had a name for Camp X, but "Camp X" itself was not one of them. The name "Camp X" was given by the locals at the time of its construction when they first became aware of the mysterious goings on behind the barbed wire. Could it be that the SD (Sicherheitsdienst), the German intelligence agents, got so close to Camp X that they believed the actual name of the Camp to be "Camp X" because the locals living in the surrounding area referred to it as such?

It is not unrealistic that the Germans were aware of Camp X. We now know that German records captured by the Allies at the end of the War clearly indicate that the Germans were aware of every aspect of the English Camp, Beaulieu, right down to the name of Lord Montagu's dog. The Montagu family owned the Beaulieu Estate.

63. *The Camp's security was not always up to par. This newspaper was destined for a Mr.Frank Baker in May of 1942. Many of the overflow of visiting dignitaries were housed at the 'Oshawa House Upon receiving the newspaper at the Oshawa House, and not having a Frank Baker registered there, the manager returned the paper to the Post office suggesting that they might,* ***"Try Camp X"***

64. Agents practice climbing the bluffs at Camp X.
(The agents can be seen at bottom left and centre of the picture.)

George Allin recalled working in his brother's field which was on the east side of Thorton Road. He hid in the dense grass by the side of the road and watched the agents down by the lake placing trip wires across the road. As a car would come down the road, it would set the charge off as it passed by. Not enough of a charge was placed to do any damage, but enough to illustrate what could happen if this were done in a real scenario and how easy it would be to blow up the car and its occupants.

At the end of a rigorous day of training, the agent would return, totally exhausted, to his room for some relaxation. Upon entering, he might notice that something was missing or misplaced. This taught him the extreme importance of observation. A mental note of the situation was recorded for future reference should it ever become an issue in a future training lecture.

In the morning, exercises were led by very tough instructors, the majority of whom were from England. Andy remembered one in particular, a very proud Scot who always wore his kilt. Another, who had already served in Europe, had a limp but was a bright, wise, and clever instructor.

The Scot instructor once said, "I'm going to go to Churchill and tell him to give us one hundred Hungarians and one hundred Scots and together we are going to F_ _ _ Hitler." He was truly fond of the Hungarian lads. Andy thought that they and the instructors shared a peasant background which made them able to relate to each other. There was also some mysterious "seventh sense" which bound them. The Hungarians were believed to be ideally suited for the Secret Service because they demonstrated a relentless determination, great stamina and held strong political beliefs.

After the war, Colonel F. H. Walter, O.B.E. (Order of the British Empire), said; *"It was only at a later stage that it was realized by Special Forces and by the British military authorities generally that the national resistance movements in themselves were powerful potential military forces. From that time forward the SF agent ceased to be merely a saboteur and became, in addition, a liaison officer and an expert in weapon training, in supply, in tactics and in leadership."*

Andy and his mates were recruited and trained for guerrilla warfare. At the Camp, the emphasis for them was on tough physical training. A typical maneuver might entail running full out and jumping off the towering cliffs to the lake below, then climbing back up from the shore to the highest point of the cliff by rope. Only nine of the original twenty-two completed the rigorous training and went on to the next phase. The intelligence training, initiated at Camp X and continued in England, prepared them not as spies but as agents.

(Author's Note: During my investigation of Camp X, I had been told that one of the reasons the Whitby shoreline of Lake Ontario had been chosen was due to the uncanny similarity of the beach front to the shores of France, gradually sloping southward toward the thirty foot high cliffs. In a later interview with Tommy Drew-Brook, head of the Canadian Division of the BSC, I learned that this, in fact, had nothing to do with the decision to pick this particular site. The coincidence of the similarity did make it extremely convenient, however.)

Live ammunition was used in all practices. No one shot directly at the agents-in-training of course, but the stress of knowing that live ammunition was being fired your way added to the sense of realism and reinforced the seriousness of the exercise. It was survival training in its truest sense. It taught the agent to keep his head, but at the same time made him angry and determined.

The agent-in-training also concentrated on demolition; factories, railways, bridges and locomotives were frequent and logical targets. On one such exercise, Andy and his fellow agents were in the Toronto railway yards (Union Station) where they decided to 'steal' a locomotive. One of the men asked the others whether anyone knew how to operate it and the answer was unanimously, "no". After careful consideration, and in spite of this minor detail, the decision was made to proceed anyway. They managed to get the train moving down the line, but could not figure out how to switch it. Soon they realized that there was a train approaching them on what appeared to be the same line. They quickly jumped from the train and ran as far and as fast as they could to avoid the explosion from the expected inevitable collision. But the train carried on, slowing down, until it gently bumped another train and came to an uneventful stop. The agents, upon returning to the Camp, informed their instructor what had transpired. The proper authorities were immediately dispatched to Union Station to explain to the manager just what had happened and to instruct him to consider the damage as the Station's part of the war effort. He received no further explanation.

As long as these exercises were properly executed and no one was injured, there was never any objection from the Camp instructors. There was always someone available from the Camp to serve as "damage control" after the agents had left the scene, and the agents knew that the Camp authorities would always cover their tracks.

Of necessity, the Camp had devised quite a unique plan of action in the event that one of their agents got into trouble. It was essential that the Camp be able to locate and retrieve the agent, as well as to satisfactorily explain his actions.

On one particular training mission, one of the trainees was apprehended and the police were called in. When the agent was confronted with hand cuffs, he requested that the RCMP be contacted with a message: "S25-1-1" (the secret RCMP file number for Camp X). Inquisitively but reluctantly, the policeman phoned and relayed the message. Within fifteen minutes, an RCMP officer was on the scene and told the policeman that he would take care of the incident and that if the police had any further questions they should contact Inspector McLellan at RCMP H.Q. Within the hour, the agent found himself back at Camp X.

The agents "hit" many local targets, including General Motors in Oshawa, the port of Toronto and especially the Toronto/Montreal rail line. Andy could not recall the number of times they simulated blow ups of trains using fake plastique (RDX) explosive developed by the BSC at Ajax (DIL) and Camp X. After a few such attacks, the "doomed" engineers would spot the agents lying in the long grass by the tracks and throw up their hands, knowing what was in store for them and suspecting that the men by the tracks were either local patriots getting ready for the invasion, or subversives-in-training.

(Author's Note: One can only imagine what the engineers told their supervisors upon their return at the end of the run. It is amazing to think that, to the best of our knowledge, no formal complaints were ever lodged against the Camp by the CPR (Canadian Pacific Railway). Or perhaps there were, but if so, the complaints never saw the light of day.)

Agents learned that derailment caused the enemy some headaches, but could be repaired in a few hours and really proved to be little more than a nuisance. A truly effective delay could be caused by taking out a site such as a bridge or a viaduct which could potentially take days to reconstruct and required a greater number of personnel to complete, a recurring objective in the training program.

Killing the enemy was in order when in a kill-or-be-killed situation; otherwise, it was far better to merely injure a man. By doing so, other able-bodied men were kept from entering combat as their services would be required in various support tasks to assist in tending to the wounded personnel. Instead of taking out only one of the enemy, several could be removed from combat at the same time.

Plastique was a brilliant invention. It could be coloured to conceal it from detection and it could be formed into any shape. With a fuse and an ignition timer, it could be set then left to blow at a later time; in two hours or two weeks, "BOOM!" One half a pound could cut a steel train rail like butter. Near the camp, there were some hydro transformers on which the agents practiced placing and detonating plastique.

(Author's Note: The reason for not having tall fences covered with vines now becomes evident. Even if curious eyes were able to see inside the Camp, they could not see anything out of the ordinary. All activity was conducted inside the unassuming buildings; silent killing training was conducted inside one barn, small arms training in another barn, class room theory was taught in the Lecture Hall, secrets were being transmitted from inside Hydra, and confidential strategy meetings were being held in the C.O.'s residence. Even if someone were to get within a hundred yards of the Camp, they would not be able to see anything confidential, secret or even unusual.)

To be able to shoot a target with a revolver or a pistol from a distance of twenty feet required much practice and training, most of which was carried out in the underground firing range. There was not a ray of light, not even the light of the moon. Shooting had to be by instinct, by sensing movements, even perhaps utilizing the sense of smell. There was no option - the agent must hit the target, he HAD to. He was trained, "grilled, almost tortured mentally until he hit that target." That was all there was. It was just part of the training.

"The night maneuvers were bloody awful", recounted Andy Daniels. The agents would be taken by Jeep to the area around Orono, or perhaps to Rice Lake, near Peterborough. They would be given a map and compass, told their target and left to find their way back, completing the mission. "Meanwhile, the instructors would sit playing cards, or sipping a beer, waiting."

When the agents arrived on target, hours later, they would be loaded into a Jeep, tired and hungry, and would head for Camp. As often as not, though, they would not reach Camp, but would be "told that there was a new 'situation', be given their new targets and they would stagger off in all directions to fulfill yet another mission."

On night maneuvers, they would sometimes land a little Tiger Moth in the open field on the far side of Corbett Creek. The trainees would then have to scramble through the brush and be on board in less than a minute. This particular training maneuver began for Andy when he was selected to practice entering enemy territory as a secret agent. The rest of the group were to be resistance members. Andy was taken to Oshawa airport and put in a Tiger Moth which landed a few feet outside the Camp fence directly across Corbett Creek from the buildings. The receiving party, other agents in the role of resistance fighters, was waiting for him, and together they would 'infiltrate' the Camp. The Camp guards were awaiting them but the 'Partisans' eluded them by crawling to their target, one of the Camp buildings, and laying a charge. Andy and the others retreated having succeeded in their "mission".

65. A Tiger Moth, useful for its quick take-off and landing capability

The timing of each guard watch was never routine but always random. The guard never made a perimeter check at the same time after the hour as did the previous watch. This, of course, was by design in order that any observer would not be able to predict when a guard would pass by any given check point on his watch, thus making it more difficult for any would-be infiltrator.

One evening, Private Bailey and Mac McDonald, having just completed their rounds of the camp, were sitting in the guard house having a cigarette. Private Bailey said that he was feeling restless and wanted to go for a walk. He had just started down the old farm road toward the Camp when he saw a man appear from the bushes at the side of the road and walk toward him.

Bailey was understandably alarmed and automatically clicked into the routine calling out, "Who goes there?" There was no response. Bailey drew his .45 pistol from his holster and pointed it toward the person. He gave another warning. Again Bailey received no response. As he had been trained to do, he fired his gun.

Back in the guard house, Mac had started to worry about Bailey as he had been gone longer than he had said he would be. Mac had left the guard house and started to walk down the road toward Camp when he heard the gun shot. As he got closer, he could see Bailey walking toward him, accompanied by another man. As they approached, Mac said to Bailey, "Did you fire your gun?" Mac could now see the other man with Bailey and was surprised to see that it was Captain Millman, the Camp doctor. Mac could also see that Bailey was white as a ghost.

Mac asked, "What happened?"

Doctor Millman snapped back, "I'm lucky to be alive, that's what happened!" For some reason Doctor Millman had not heard the warnings of Private Bailey.

Bailey said, "Thank God my gun jammed," of course saving Doctor Millman's life.

The next morning, after the incident had been reported, Commanding Officer Brooker ordered an inquiry and extensive testing to be done on Bailey's gun. The results of the test on the .45 showed that, of the remaining bullets in the chamber, all five fired perfectly. Doctor Millman had literally dodged a bullet.

* * *

The Hungarian agents' training took about ten weeks to complete that summer of 1943. They had landed at Camp X sometime in the middle of June, and they departed in the last days of August. All in all, it was very rigorous, extensive training and they emerged from Camp X hardened beyond any other military, physical, mental or emotional experience that they would endure in life.

66. Andy (top right) and his secret agent mates at Bari, Italy, 1944

Directly from Camp X, the agents were shipped overseas on the "Queen Elizabeth." When they arrived in Glasgow, there were twenty two thousand troops on board the ship. Andy remembers that they had to sleep in three shifts and, if you did not get any sleep on your shift, you were out of luck.

They were all dressed in Canadian uniforms, complete with Canadian insignia. No one had any idea that they were secret agents as they looked exactly the same as any of the other thousands of soldiers on board.

Training continued at another SOE school in Scotland. Andy was then shipped out to Cairo where he had his first chance to test his skills learned in the weeks of preparation at Camp X. He wandered into a bar and sat down at a table alone. Shortly after ordering, he was joined by a friendly chap who wanted to talk and buy him drinks. A few well-placed questions on Andy's part soon convinced him that the man was not quite what he presented. Andy determined that he was an Abwehr Agent (German Military Intelligence) and was also certain that he knew Andy's identity as well. The drinking began in earnest. Anyone watching them would have thought they were a couple of drunken soldiers, what with the quantity of booze they were each putting away. Damned if Andy did not outlast him, though. He literally drank his companion under the table. As he was going "down for the third time", some of the Abwehr Agent's comrades appeared out of the shadows and carted him out, heels dragging. Never before, nor since, had Andy drunk so much. His hangover lasted a week!

From there the agents went to Bari, Italy, to prepare for their missions and take a well deserved rest, exactly what they would need when one considers what was in store for them. Regarding Bari, Italy, Eric Curwain would later write, *"Our special Signals Unit in Bari was administered from a building next to a church and had everything a field office of that type should have; photography unit for faking documents, engraving and printing equipment, coding and decoding staff. Attached was a radio interception and transmitting station to maintain contact with agents in Yugoslavia, northern Italy, Austria and Hungary and with our Ops. Room at headquarters in England.*

"There was also a school for training agents in Morse and in the use of mobile field transmitters. One of the instructors was an Italian who had returned from a mission with his finger nails mutilated by his German captors when he had landed from his canoe at the wrong spot on the Adriatic coast near Ancona.

"There was a store of foreign-type clothing for agents dropping into countries of which they were usually native or linguistically suited to pass as such. It contained a strange collection of gadgets and stores for the use of parachute types (sic), ranging from currency to whiskey, cigarettes, to fly buttons containing tiny compasses and beautiful maps printed in silk. When the Germans discovered that men's fly buttons hid compasses which screwed into one half of the button, the British inventors reversed the thread and this fooled the Germans into believing the buttons were normal, since they could not unscrew them by turning them in the usual direction."

* * *

Andy came out of his thoughtful stupor and resumed looking at the flashing red light. The dispatcher stood by the door having already performed half of his duties in preparing Andy and the others by hooking up their static lines. Andy was just as glad that the dispatcher had hooked him up because he was too nervous to do it himself.

They were flying over Hungary, at well above twenty three thousand feet. Andy could hear the anti-aircraft artillery booming all around the Halifax and he prayed that one would not hit the plane. They were, in fact, too high to be in range, but Andy and the others could not know that at the time. Andy could see the ack-ack bursting all around the drop chute. He recalled that it looked like Christmas lights to him.

As the Halifax approached its target, the amber, solid, 'stand by' light came on. This is it, Andy thought. There was no stopping now. All of his training would lead to this one jump. The time was near. Soon the light would turn green. "Right lads, come on now, let's get ready", barked out the dispatcher.

Andy thought, "You have to be either drunk or crazy to jump out of an aircraft at this altitude, perhaps into the arms of the enemy."

Each of the men had a number which designated the jump sequence. Andy was number two. Number one was Major 'S', an Irish Catholic. He had never touched alcohol. Never. Andy and the others were each allowed a flask of rum to carry in their jump suits. It would help to keep them warm and would make the trip down a little easier, Andy thought. Major 'S' had turned his down.

Finally, the 'green' light came on; it was time. Andy pulled out his flask of rum and went to take another swallow. Just as he put the flask to his mouth, Major 'S' said, "Give me that!," grabbed the flask from Andy and downed the rest of the contents in a mighty gulp!

67. An SOE agent in his parachute jumpsuit and helmet

"Time!," yelled out the dispatcher. With that, Major 'S' was gone from the airplane, as though he had never been there. "Right then, number two, you're out!" In the fraction of a second before Andy jumped, number three gave him a swallow from his flask. It was greatly appreciated.

Half way down, Andy realized that he was stone cold sober and, by the time he reached the ground, he was as cold as death. But the biggest surprise was still to come. "Someone had miscalculated!" Just on the other side of the hill, about a mile away, were the Germans. Andy thought to himself, "This is not a good beginning for my first mission," and he struggled to cut his shroud lines. He had gone from the relative safety of the Halifax, twenty three thousand feet in the air, to sitting in the middle of a hornets nest on the ground. As he struggled to get out of his overalls, he could hear the slightly off-sync drone of the Halifax's engines; minutes later he was free of the lines and his parachute.

"Several more minutes passed before he found his jump-mates, one of whom, an expert map reader, informed them that they were lost! Although later evidence was to prove him correct, this intelligence was not at all well received at that particular moment.

"Readers who have examined the appendices in *SOE In France* will perhaps be familiar with the instructions which were given to pilots engaged in dropping agents, to the effect that navigation by visual ground references at night can be terribly misleading. The author of these *Notes For Pilots,* Wing Commander H. S. Verity, DSO, DFC, reports that he became confused as to which of two villages he had approached, and spent 'two miserable hours' trying to sort things out.

"The error later proved to be even greater than he had anticipated by some eighteen kilometers! However, with the enemy only metres away, there was nothing for the agents to do but to find shelter and get some rest before attempting to straighten themselves out. Accordingly, they spent a miserable night huddled together in the woods. At daybreak they decided that it would be best to split up. They did so, with the understanding that they would meet up some time later at a safe house in Budapest."

As he traveled from village to village, Andy became increasingly aware that the Germans were closing in. There were soldiers everywhere. His brain automatically clicked into training mode and he ducked into an abandoned building, changed into his priest's vestments and continued safely on his way, blending inconspicuously into the local populace.

Andy determined that his best course was to seek out a 'halfway' safe house, in a small village along the route, but in his haste to find sanctuary, he very nearly blew his months of training. "Upon arriving at the correct address, he mounted the front steps in his best 'homme du monde' manner, and rang the doorbell. In a moment, he was greeted by a lady and he inquired for her husband. She stepped back, visibly shaken. After what seemed like an eternity, she said that her husband had been dead for six months."

68. Andy Durovecz (Daniels) prepares for his mission at Bari, Italy, 1944

For a moment, Andy was unable to explain her behaviour to himself. Then, it suddenly occurred to him that he "had not given her any of the pre-arranged passwords. He was mortified. He had failed his very first test. In his confusion, he muttered the words and, just as he turned to leave, she motioned to him to enter."

Gratefully, he followed her into the house and she closed the door behind him. "For months, she said, she had been rehearsing the code words, in the expectation of Andy's arrival. His direct inquiry for her deceased husband threw her into a panic. Was Andy the Gestapo? In one agonizing moment she had, 'evaluated your veracity, and decided to trust you', she said."

"Andy remained there for several days. They became quite fond of one another, but he eventually left to meet his comrades."

On his return to Hungary in 1979, as he tried to retrace each step of his mission, he found himself on those same steps, thirty-six years later. His anticipation of a joyous reunion knew no bounds. But the door was opened by a stranger. "No", she said, "Mrs. ... doesn't live here anymore".

The response to his request for her new address hit him like a hammer blow: "Mrs. ... was taken by the Gestapo, in 1944. We think she died in Belsen. They said that she had been found guilty of harbouring a British secret agent."

After the war, Andy wrote to England inquiring about information on himself for his now published book, "*My Secret Mission*". The reply;

"*You joined STS 103, in mid 1943...You arrived in England on 18 September, 1943. Here you continued your training as a W/T operator and sabotage agent in various SOE Training Schools. You proceeded to Cairo in February, 1944. In May you were transferred to Italy. From Bari you were parachuted on 18 September, 1944, in the name of Lieutenant Andrew Daniels, into Slovakia, with three other officers, to establish contact with the Slovak Headquarters at Banska Bystrica which was organizing the Slovak rising.*"

69. The Halifax Bomber, transport for many agents to their various missions

70. The agents taking their finishing Parachute training—
note the special drop-hole in the plane

"There you were instructed to cross into Hungary in civilian clothes to make a reconnaissance and obtain papers and safe addresses to which the other three officers could eventually proceed. You crossed the frontier on 19 October and reached Budapest safely. But as it proved impossible to obtain the necessary papers, you decided to return to Slovakia to rejoin the three officers at Banska Bystrica. However, when attempting to re-cross the frontier, you were arrested and imprisoned by the Hungarians. By the end of October 1944, the Slovak rising had been suppressed by the Germans and the three other officers had escaped into the hills, where they were subsequently also arrested.

"You remained in Hungarian prisons at Misols and in Habik where you met the SOE-trained Mike Turk and 'G.' You succeeded in escaping and remained in hiding in Budapest until it was occupied by the Russians. They evacuated you, thus enabling you to proceed, via Italy, to England. You arrived in London on 23 May, 1945, and returned to Canada on 7 June, 1945."

After some time, Andy was transferred from the prison to a temporary internment camp. Andy and the others were on their way to one of the death camps inside the Reich. Andy escaped during his fourth night at the new camp. It was a dreary, rainy night. Andy and his fellow captives were allowed to get some wood for a fire, but it was wet. They plugged up the pipes of their heater, lit the fire with the wet wood which began to smoke heavily, and as the guards ran into the room, they slipped out the side door and made their way back to safety.

After the war, Andy returned to Hungary for the purpose of doing research for his book. He tried to re-enter the place where he had been imprisoned by the Hungarian Counter Espionage and the Gestapo at the time when the Red Army was getting near. They would not let him enter as it was still a military barracks at that time. He had hoped to be able to find some record of his stay there, but to no avail. All records had been destroyed by the Gestapo when the Red Army was approaching. For two days and nights, they had burned the records in the courtyard where previously the executions had taken place.

Andy returned to Camp X one cold November day in 1977. I was his guide this time as I was more informed regarding the current condition of the Camp than was Andy. As mentioned earlier, at this time all that was left of the Camp were the concrete foundations. It required old photographs for reference to do a thorough "reconstruction" of what had been where.

"So this is Camp X," said Andy, as he looked around the barren fields, his eyes piercing through the overgrown grass in search of ghosts in the shadows. "There," he said, pointing toward the south east and Lake Ontario. "That's where a good part of our training took place; the explosives. I remember the Sunday afternoons we had off. We would play football (soccer) for hours. The Camp trainers loved it because the physical training was great for us. Those damned craters!," said Andy. "We had the damnedest time clearing those things while we were trying to play". The craters were of course caused by the explosions of the previous day's training.

As he told me, the one thing that he remembered most out of all of his training, was the open field 'evasive' exercise. "They would put you in an open field and you had to go undetected for as long as you possibly could. The way to do this and be undetected was to remain perfectly still as it is difficult to see an unmoving target. If you moved and were spotted, a round of fire over your head would signify that you had been spotted".

The other thing that Andy always remembered was how he was taught to 'take a man out.' They would teach the agent, "Do not go for the testicles from the front, go for them by way of the back which puts you in better control." And finally, "Stick your fingers into their, ears, eyes or nose with full force as the individual must give this his full attention giving you time to 'finish him off.'"

Andy gazed in the other direction, north toward the trees that still lined the original roads. He thought back to the cold, dark prison where he had been interred after he had been captured. He thought about the torture and the constant interrogations. After all, that was where he had lost his innocence. Life had been so much simpler here at the Camp. Even in the most rigorous times in the training program, if you made a mistake, someone was quick to point it out to you and everything could be taken back or done over.

Upon Andy's return to Toronto, he settled down and got married. Unfortunately, all his years of training and his experiences as a secret agent would eventually take the inevitable toll on Andy as on so many others; not just the agents, but anyone who had lived through or served in the war. It seemed perhaps to affect the agents more than others because of the type of training that they had been through.

As was understandable, Andy did not want to talk with his new bride about his experiences during the war. As a result, when his behaviour began to change later on, she had no idea how to cope. Andy began to have terrible nightmares of being captured by the Gestapo and about the subsequent torture he had endured. To someone who has never experienced such treatment, you can only try to imagine yourself laying flat on a board, nude, and having live electrical wires attached to your testicles. Should you not answer the interrogators' questions to their liking, they would flip the switch. Try to imagine also knowing that you would continue to receive increasingly stronger jolts as long as you persisted in giving unsatisfactory answers until either you gave in or passed out. To Andy, this had been reality.

Andy's nightmares became more frequent as time went on, but still he could not disclose the torment he suffered. He would jump out of bed in a cold sweat in the middle of the night. His wife tried to understand, but never knew what caused his violent behaviour. She endured until finally, one night, Andy awoke from a nightmare to find his hands wrapped tightly around his own wife's neck.

This was the end of Andy's marriage. He never remarried.

Andy died alone in 1998.

* * *

Trained along with Andy at Camp X was a man named Joe Gelleny. Joe was only twenty years old when, while working as a lab technician in Toronto, he decided to join the Canadian Army.

"I was looking for some type of adventure, but not quite to this degree!" His application to the paratroopers was quickly approved and stamped "Hold — Important". During an RCMP review, the appraiser noticed that the box entitled, "Languages?" was answered, "fluent Hungarian." The next thing Joe knew, he was called in for an interview by the SOE for "special work".

After much vetting and discussion, Joe found himself at Camp X where he would meet Andy Daniels, ten years his senior. Even though Joe and Andy trained together, each was never allowed to know what the other's assignment would be. In the event that one of them were ever to be captured, he would not be able to disclose his comrade's mission.

After his "Finishing School" training and final briefing at Bari, Italy, Joe was sent on his mission to build "pockets" of resistance and to train the Partisans in acts of sabotage.

Like the others, Joe Gelleny was parachuted into Yugoslavia and quickly picked up by his pre-arranged resistance group, one of which included among its members one Sterling Hayden, a famous Hollywood movie star. Hayden was with the American OSS which was strongly entrenched in the Balkans. Hayden's responsibility was to receive supplies for the Partisans, and to assist Allied flyers out of Europe.

After his capture Joe was moved from one prison to another. Emaciated, he wondered what his fate would be: he had lost fifty pounds and was being tortured almost daily. By this time, Andy Daniels had also been captured and was being moved from prison to prison. The fact that both Andy and Joe were captured in their uniforms probably saved their lives.

Eventually, Andy was transferred to Hadik military prison, the last stop before being sent off to the concentration camp at Buchenwald. Then something startling happened; "About a week after my arrival, I heard sounds which suggested the prisoners were being exercised. Soon it seemed that the voices were being addressed to me and I discerned the frequent repetition of the word 'Partisan'. I recognized the voices of my Canadian mates, John Coates, Mike Turk and Joe Gelleny. It had been circulated that they were prisoners here, but hearing them gave me renewed strength and confidence. I wondered why they used "Partisan" as a password. Anxious to see them, I climbed the bunk and, in a running jump, so to speak, I leapt up and grabbed hold of the bars on the window. All I could do was to identify myself by a shout."

Andy deduced why his friends Mike Turk and Joe Gelleny kept using the code word, "Partisan." Turk and Gelleny were aware that Andy had been brought to the same prison and they were trying to communicate to him that, from what they had witnessed, if you were dressed in military uniform and you declared yourself to simply be a "Partisan." then you had a better chance of surviving. It would also serve to keep the Gestapo off the true track.

On December 12, 1944, Joe Gelleny and others made their escape from Zugliget prison. They sought out the safe houses along their route which they had memorized and, after many close calls, finally found their destination. While in hiding, Joe was not content to just sit and wait. He continued to produce forged documents to help fleeing Jews. There were numerous close calls while stowed in the safe house. The Germans would burst their way in without notice in search for Resistance people and pull them outside. By day, Joe could only sit back and watch the slaughter going on in the streets of Budapest.

On January 20, 1945, the sounds of war were silenced in the streets. People mingled about talking and laughing like children. What had happened? The Germans had retreated and Hungary had been liberated by the Russians!

Joe was picked up by the Russians and interrogated once again.

Eventually, he was released and managed to link up with his comrades and make it safely back to England, where he was interrogated one final time.

From there, Joe returned home safely to Toronto where he lives a good life in retirement. Joe kept in touch with Andy until Andy's death in the fall of 1998 and, in fact, for all of those years lived only a few miles away from Andy yet maintained his distance. One can only wonder if what the two men had endured during the War had anything to do with why they never resumed their association even though they lived out their lives in such close proximity.

* * *

In 1943, the SOE began to hear stories regaling the strength of the Resistance group in Yugoslavia under the direction of the Partisan leader, Marshal Tito. The British decided to send a group of agents to Yugoslavia to serve as an exploratory team to determine whether or not it would be helpful to send experienced, trained agents able to build upon Tito's existing resistance group.

The British spy masters were surprised by the immediacy with which they received radio messages from their agents dropped into Yugoslavia. Of course the Yugoslav Partisans and Resistance groups would more than welcome the support of the British agents!

The next step was to assemble a group of experienced and seasoned agents for this particular mission. It was most important to indicate to Tito that the SOE were indeed serious about the prospect of assembling an army of Resistance fighters with the purpose of defeating the Nazis.

71. The proud Yugoslaves of Camp X

While the training of these agents was going on back in Canada, Tito's life in the mountains was a day to day uncertainty. In 1943 he found himself and his Resistance fighters on the verge of collapse. He spent the first half of that year in the mountains of Yugoslavia, trying to stay alive, while the Germans got ever closer. He desperately tried to avoid the real threat of total defeat for his warriors. Because of these uncertainties, Tito was protected at all times by a personal bodyguard and he carried a pistol and hand grenades, always at the ready in the event of a surprise attack by his Nazi hunters.

In the spring of 1943, Tito was nearly killed when artillery hit their encampment killing many of his Partisans while just missing him. Ironically, his dog saved his life by causing him to kneel down to find out why the dog was asking for attention. Tito's dog took most of the impact from the percussion which saved his master's life.

Even when times appeared blackest, Tito was never down and was always in good spirits. He found it necessary to continuously perk up the troops with profound words of encouragement. So often, things looked so dismally bleak that it appeared they would never survive. He would tell his fighters that they must never give up hope and they must fight to the last man and woman.

Tito was more of a father and a friend to the Partisan fighters. He was always helping them, advising them and offering words of encouragement. Tito's simple way of doing things, his compassion to the men and women, and his fearlessness in the face of the enemy brought hundreds of new resistance volunteers from the surrounding towns and villages. Word of the great leader spread quickly and it was Tito's carisma that eventually turned his fighters into an army of thousands!

With the training of this group of 'crack' Yugoslav agents completed, the team took off for Yugoslavia to link up with Tito's troops bunkered in the Yugoslav mountains. As they approached their drop zone, the agents could see the dark mountains off in the distance. The fires burning on the ground below served as the pre-arranged signal that the partisans were awaiting them. One by one, as they jumped from the plane, the agents found the ever-organized Yugoslavs there to greet them and their reception went off like clockwork.

The following morning, after a short trek, the SOE agents found themselves amid the camp establishment of Partisans in the mountains. Within minutes, the group faced Marshal Tito himself who was extremely happy to see them. At that time, Tito needed all the help that he could muster. He wasted no time in asking the agents how quickly they could secure and provide for his resistance group the necessary arms for the sabotage plan that was already in progress.

Radio communications flew back and forth between the agents and their home base in London. In just a matter of days, the first shipment of armaments was on its way to the Resistance group. As always, a pre-arranged drop zone was given to the British controllers advising them as to where the receiving team would be waiting.

It turned out that the timing of the agents' landing among the Partisans was more critical than they had anticipated as they soon discovered that the Germans were honing in on the location of their Camp. One evening, shortly after their arrival, Tito informed the men that he had received information from his scouts that the Germans were close by with a division of soldiers and that they must move out immediately. As they rushed to break camp, firing began and one of the SOE agents was killed. The remaining men in the group, including Marshal Tito, would live to fight another day.

72. Camp X from the air looking East. Note General Motors in the distance

The Yugoslav Partisans trained in Canada at Camp X did a marvelous job completing their assignments. According to the SOE after the war, the Yugoslavs were the most successful group of agents trained for their organization. They destroyed German railway tracks, trains, roads, telephone cables and anything else that they could blow up in order to hinder the Nazi war machine. The German soldiers, and even Hitler himself, were becoming frustrated by the successes of the Yugoslav Partisans. Hitler could not bring himself to accept the fact that the Yugoslav citizens would actually raise weapons against the German people.

These Partisans were so good at fulfilling their assignments that they eventually turned the Nazis' own weapons back on themselves by using captured bombs and guns in the execution of their missions. On the occasions when the Partisans cut the German telephone lines, they would always take the extracted wire with them so that the wires could not be repaired. Instead, this forced the Germans to go back for replacement wire which, of course, meant that the vital lines would be down for days.

Eventually, the Partisans became so brazen as to hide along the roadsides and wait in the bushes until a German patrol would come down the road. They then would strike out with the cold blooded speed of a snake, swiftly and silently killing all of their unsuspecting victims. It was this type of sabotage that the secret agents were taught at Camp X and that would become so valuable to the war effort and the eventual defeat of the Nazis.

* * *

French Canadians were natural candidates for Camp X and the SOE. They were certainly an obvious choice for action in France. Two such agents were Major L. G. (Guy) D'Artois and Captain R. J. Taschereau. After their preliminary training at Camp X, and subsequent training in Britain, Major D'Artois and Captain Taschereau proceeded to their assignment areas. Major D'Artois so impressed his instructors at Camp X that they could not wait to advise Britain of his expertise.

73. Left to right: Major Art Bushell, Adjutant-Quartermaster; Lieutenant-Colonel R.M. Brooker, Commandant; Major Cuthbert Skilbeck, Chief Instuctor; Captain Fred Milner, Demolition Expert

During his parachute jump training at Manchester, England, D'Artois met a woman agent, Sonia Butt, who was in his class. He fell in love with Sonia virtually immediately and, while on a day pass, they were quietly married. D'Artois begged Colonel Maurice Buckmaster, Head of the SOE "F" (for "France") Section, to let them go on their missions together.

Buckmaster told them in no uncertain terms that this was totally out of the question! If they were to be caught by the Gestapo, the Germans would take great delight in torturing Sonia in front of Guy believing that this would be the one form of torture that no man could withstand and that he would surely tell all to save his wife.

D'Artois, by this time fondly known as "Michele le Canadien," was dropped into France one moonlit evening in 1944, not by a Halifax this time but very quietly in a Lysander. The Lysanders were famous for their short landing and take off capability. Andy Durovecz once described take offs and landings in a similar plane, a Tiger Moth, at Camp X, "The plane dropped to the ground and stopped in seconds. I had no sooner jumped out and turned to give the 'thumbs up' and the plane was fifteen feet away, taking off. They were the best planes in the business for this type of thing."

D'Artois' mission, like many others, was to meet up with the Resistance leaders whom he would find in the hills. Guy was well received and through hard work and many successes, advanced to lead three battalions of Resistance fighters, a force of approximately two thousand troops! He not only led the sabotage units but was also instrumental in the ultimate capture of over one hundred Nazi collaborators.

Many of the Resistance fighters in his group were women recruited from the local villages. D'Artois actually raised over one million francs via the ingenious method of capturing wealthy collaborators deemed to be very important to the Axis side. This new-found wealth was poured back into the Resistance organization and provided innumerable weapons and ammunition.

Shortly after Guy was dropped into France, Sonia jumped by parachute from a Halifax bomber and landed right in a "nest" of German soldiers. The receiving Resistance party quickly got her changed into peasant's clothes, allowing her to blend in nicely among the locals.

Sonia, along with another agent, Chris Hudson, went on to train hundreds of Maquis in the use of weapons and in the art of sabotage, all of which the Maquis put to good use in the liberation of Paris. After the liberation, Sonia met up with her husband and each of them went on yet another assignment behind enemy lines. These two agents would complete their separate missions and eventually return to England where Guy convinced his wife that Canada was the ideal place for them to make their new life. Shortly after, the war ended and Guy and Sonia sailed for Canada.

Captain Taschereau's assignment and subsequent completion of his mission was almost as exciting as D'Artois'. He was dropped literally into the middle of a fierce battle between the Resistance and the German troops and eventually went on to head one of the now famous Maquis of the Second World War. In one such battle, he and the troops managed to eliminate over three hundred German soldiers compared to the fewer than fifty Maquis dead. Taschereau was also successful in building a reliable drop area network where tons of supplies could be delivered on a regular basis, supplies which were invaluable in the destruction of the Axis movement. Eventually, the SOE found it essential to recall Taschereau to England as they could ill afford the capture of this most valuable agent.

* * *

Were anyone to make light of the seriousness of this training, all one need do is note the fate of three Canadian agents in particular. Although, in fact, their training may not have actually taken place at Camp X, their fate might just as easily have been shared by any of the many agents trained at any of the SOE schools.

Captain J. K. McAllister, Lieutenant H. F. Pickersgill and Lieutenant R. Sabourin were three agents from a group of eight who had been dropped into the Ardennes; their mission, to sabotage important targets in their selected arena of war. At the time of their recruitment, McAllister was already in England. Ironically, Pickersgill had been studying in France when the war broke out and had been captured by the Germans shortly after they invaded France.

Pickersgill was sent to a prison at St. Denis from which he eventually escaped and was quickly rescued by the Resistance who secured his passage back to England. Upon his safe return, Pickersgill, with an understandable sense of animosity toward the Germans resulting from the treatment which he had received at their hands, quickly joined the Special Forces of the SOE where he served with McAllister. Unfortunately for the two young Canadians, they were dropped into a controlled circuit and were quickly captured and taken to the Gestapo Headquarters in Paris which sealed their fate.

The Germans had been playing back the circuits' "pianos" for some time. 'Funkspiel' was the German word for sending messages to England on radio transmitters which had been captured along with their operators. The captive agent, at gunpoint, would "practice" transmitting a dictated message on his own frequency and with his own recognizable secret code name, obviously intended to lead the incoming agents into a trap. A German radio operator would sit beside him and mimic his speed and touch until he could replicate both, hence the term "piano", then would transmit the signal himself on the agent's radio in order that the British would think that all was well.

Many years later Eric Curwain would say the following about 'Funkspiel,' *"Prior to returning to Canada in early 1942, I had suggested to the SOE*

that before any agent trained by our unit in Canada (Camp X) be sent over-
seas into the field his 'fist' should be tape recorded, that is, his style of using
the Morse key. When an agent was captured, the first step of the enemy was
to force him to keep up his radio contact with home base. His captors knew
that his training would include the use of certain transmission or encoding
tricks but these tricks could be detected and if he refused to give absolute
co-operation, he was executed.

"In the factual report entitled Operation North Pole, the chief of the
German counter-intelligence stationed in Holland in 1942 and 1943 tells
how many Dutch agents from Britain were captured and used in this way.
The German author states in his report that they had expected the British to
tape-record the sending style of each agent but apparently this had not been
done and so it was easy for the Germans to use their own operators once
they had extracted from the captured Dutch agent his times of schedule,
codes and so on.

"There is, of course, the additional factor that operators at the home
base may be inattentive as my own experience in Poland proved. They may
not notice the style of sending but whenever there might be doubt, and
provided the tape record was available, the incoming transmission could
always be recorded mechanically for comparison should home base sus-
pect something wrong at the other end."

The third agent, Lieutenant R. Sabourin, was dropped a few weeks
after McAllister and Pickersgill into what the SOE believed to be a safe
circuit. They had steadily been receiving what they thought were accurate
messages from Captain Pickersgill which were, in fact, transmitted over his
confiscated radio by a German operator. Pickersgill had refused, even under torture, to co-operate. The unfortunate Sabourin was dropped directly
into the hands of the Gestapo as his parachute hit the ground. A gun battle
ensued and Lieutenant Sabourin at least had the satisfaction of killing two
Gestapo agents before being overpowered.

After torturing the three Canadians for months, the Gestapo tired of the
fact that the Canadians would not break. They ultimately sent the three to
Buchenwald where they were each put in solitary confinement to await
their fates. In September of 1944, the three Canadians, along with other
Canadians captured previously, were taken to an anteroom of the infamous
Buchenwald ovens and were unceremoniously hung on hooks mounted in
the wall while being strangled with piano wire.

The agent-in-training was certainly aware of the potential danger in
store for him in the execution of his upcoming mission. One need only read
the last letter that Frank Pickersgill wrote to his brother, Jack, back in Canada
a mere two days before he was dropped into France to sense his state of
mind as he prepared to embark.

In that letter, Frank told his brother that he was in good spirits and anxious to go on his assignment. But he also included in his letter a will that he had made out that very day. Frank also asked his brother to take care of any debts that were outstanding in his name in the event that something might happen to him.

The stories get even worse as agent after agent was dropped into these German controlled circuits. The missions, at this particular point in the war, late 1944, both pre- and post-invasion, became extremely difficult and even more dangerous than ever. First of all, the Germans had become very adept at detecting secret agents behind enemy lines and, secondly, it had now become evident to Hitler that he was losing the war. He was so infuriated that the Resistance had become as strong and as successful as it had, that he had given the order for all captured spies to be executed. Many other agents, such as a Lieutenant R. Byerly and a Captain F. A. Deniset would suffer a similar fate to that of Pickersgill, McAllister and Sabourin.

Another Camp X trained agent to be dropped into France was a Captain J. P. Archambault, along with a group of seven other agents from the U. K. They were dropped in a field in France by Lysander planes just prior to the Normandy invasion. Their mission: to "create havoc." Archambault and the others were exceptionally successful in their mission due to the fact that Hitler was preoccupied with the impending invasion. The previous successes of other agents had created pockets of Resistance which now numbered in the thousands, and who were in position to assist the agents in their endeavors.

Archambault worked primarily in the hills of France, recruiting and outfitting Resistance fighters with weapons. Training them in armed and unarmed combat became a full time exercise which he continued until linking up with the U. S. Army on their way through France. Archambault was then taken back to England where, after a thorough debriefing, he prepared for his next mission.

Captain Archambault was subsequently called upon for the Far East where experienced agents were critically needed. After a brief vacation back in Canada, Archambault and other agents went back to England to prepare for their new assignments. From England, they were taken to Ceylon for final jungle training, then to a 'staging area' in India for briefing. In early 1945, eight French Canadian agents, including Captain Archambault, were parachuted into the Karenni Region. Here, their explosives training at Camp X would serve them well as their mission was to sabotage the jungle paths used by the Japanese. It is somewhat ironic that these men operated in full uniform as there was absolutely no point in trying to disguise them. Were they to be caught, there would be no question as to their purpose for being there.

It was during the monsoon season that spring when Captain Archambault found his explosives wet and unserviceable. He did the only thing that he could, and took the explosives into his tent in an attempt to dry them. The facts get blurred at this point in that Archambault was alone when his tent blew up with him inside. He died a few days later from his extensive injuries.

Major J. H. A. (Joseph) Benoit was deployed on the fields of France with Captain Archambault and five others. Benoit was an unusual agent as he was older than most (38) and had a wife and four children at home. Benoit's most successful exploit was in the Champagne area. Not once but twice he was successful in cutting the Reims-Berlin telephone cable by soaking it with a toxic substance. He had other successes in blowing up vital supplies for the Normandy front. Benoit was also highly effective in organizing the Resistance cells and training them in the operation of rifles and other related weapons. Benoit was single-handedly responsible for advising the British as to the whereabouts of a cluster of V-1 rockets that were poised and ready for deployment against Britain. Due to Major Benoit's information, this particular group of rockets were destroyed by the Royal Air Force.

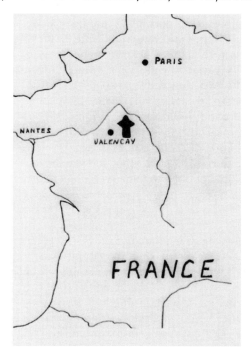

74. The SOE memorial at Valencay symbolizes occupation and liberation.
It is in this field where over 400 "F Section" agents landed in Lysander planes.
Of these, 104 died in action or at the hands of the Gestapo. The names of the 104
dead agents are each marked on the monument

Major Benoit narrowly escaped capture when his driver got intoxicated one night in a cafe and started talking about his exploits. The driver had been overheard and was taken in by the Gestapo for further questioning. Benoit managed to escape with his life.

Benoit, like many of the other French Canadians, found it difficult, upon his return to his unit, to adhere to the strict military conduct after the relative freedom he had been accustomed to all through his training and missions, so Benoit re-enlisted for another mission.

Along with Archambault and six others, Benoit was sent back into action, again in the Far East. Benoit was dropped in the spring of 1945 with Archambault and Taschereau. Benoit completed this mission in the Far East and, once again, returned to England where he promptly signed up for yet another SOE mission. He became a member of the 'Jedburgh Team' which was parachuted into Malaya to set up Resistance groups amongst the Chinese Communists, as well as to continue the sabotage of Japanese trails as before.

After three separate SOE missions behind enemy lines, Major Joseph Benoit returned to Canada and his family for a well deserved retirement.

Ralph Beauclerk was parachuted into France as a W/T radio operator. Of his mission Beauclerk said, "We had a great fear of being caught because we knew perfectly well what would happen to us, but the truth is that I enjoyed the experience immensely."

Two Canadian agents at one of the "Finishing Schools", Guy Bieler and Gabriel Chartrand, both from "F" Section, were talking generally about their upcoming missions. Guy turned to Gabriel and said, "We probably have a 50-50 chance of coming out alive."

These two quotes illustrate that indeed the agents were all too well aware of what would happen to them were they to be caught by the Gestapo.

* * *

In addition to the Canadian Yugoslavs and Hungarians trained at Camp X and who went on to missions behind enemy lines, there were also smaller groups of ethnic trainees. Among them notably are a Dane named Jen Peter Carlson, a Romanian named George Georgescu and an Italian named Vetere.

These agents each were trained to assist the Resistance movement behind enemy lines by passing on the training that he had received at Camp X. Thus, there would always be instructors instructing new instructors who in turn would train even more instructors, and so on, creating a snowball effect.

By September of 1944, the need for training special operatives in North America had greatly declined. The Camp's unique curriculum was disbanded although the communications capability continued to operate and play an important role in the war effort. As the war in Europe came to a close, the Camp's last Commandant supervised the removal of the BSC records from New York to Camp X. There the records were summarized and a number of copies printed in the Algar Press building in Oshawa under conditions of utmost security.

All the original documentation was then carefully and systematically destroyed. In 1947, the Camp X property was formally handed over to the Signal Corps of the Canadian Army. With the end of the war, most clandestine activity connected with Camp X was concluded. Its last known connection with the "Secret War" occurred when Igor Gouzenko, the young cipher clerk and, coincidentally, Russian spy, who had decided to turn himself in to the Canadian Government and seek political asylum (more in Chapter X, "The Investigation of Camp X"), was taken from Ottawa to Camp X to be kept secure under circumstances of extreme secrecy. With its communication capabilities enhanced by the Signal Corps, Camp X would later play an important role in the Korean War. In 1969, the installation was disbanded the land sold to the City of Oshawa and the Town of Whitby.

Throughout its existence, Camp X was shrouded in mystery. To those who worked there and to the local residents the Camp was to become called "Camp X". To the BSC, it was known in its early days simply as "the Camp" or "the Farm." Officially, it was designated by the Department of National Defence as file No. S25-1-1, and subsequently, as Military Research Centre No. 2. Those who worked there were only identified by a security pass citing the file No. 25-1-1 and by a bracelet bearing the same symbols. To the British , it was known as STS (Special Training School) 103.

Two things that have been now established were not generally known at the time. One, that Camp X and indeed the BSC were very largely Canadian operations, and that the significance of Camp X, in terms of the war effort, makes this site one of the most important secret military installations of the Second World War.

Lynn-Philip Hodgson

116

Chapter VII

Deaths

It is miraculous, to say the least, that given the approximately one thousand days of the Camp's life, there were so few recorded deaths which took place there. This becomes even more significant when you bear in mind that live ammunition was used exclusively, making all the demolition and firearms exercises extremely dangerous. It is inevitable, however, that there would be some fatalities from the long days of training.

August of 1942 arrived hot and unbearably humid, the kind of weather that makes breathing all but impossible and any exertion hardly worth the effort. Even along the normally cooler shores of Lake Ontario there was no relief, even at night. The moon shone so brightly that the beach was illuminated as if by floodlights and, despite the stifling heat, people could be seen scrambling, running frantically with no sense of direction or purpose. The events of this evening at Camp X had never occurred there before.

Staff Sergeant Maloney ran along the dirt roads that led to the C.O.'s residence. As he got closer, he tried to formulate in his mind exactly what he would say to the C.O. that could begin to describe what had just happened. He reached the house, threw open the screen door without knocking, and ran inside. He found the C.O. in the parlour, reading the evening paper.

The C.O. asked for an immediate explanation for his behaviour. Maloney blurted, "Come quickly, Sir. There's been an accident!"

"What kind of accident?"

"A bad accident, Sir!" he replied.

The C.O., Lieutenant-Colonel Roper-Caldbeck, called to his Quartermaster and ordered him to phone Doctor Millman immediately. Then he and Staff Sergeant Maloney ran out the door and headed toward the lake.

Bill Hardcastle was sitting at a table in the N.C.O.'s recreation room with some fellow camp personnel chatting and generally making small talk, trying to find some respite from the muggy evening. Another mate was listlessly plunking on the piano when screams could suddenly be heard over the conversation and the music. Bill ran to his room, grabbed a large flashlight, and rushed out the door heading toward the source of the screams. It seemed to take him hours to get there but, in fact, it was only a matter of a few minutes.

75. The beach at Camp X as photographed by the author in 1977

He finally reached the lake only to find a man standing there help-lessly calling out in the night over the black water. Bill recognized the man as one who worked in the Communications Building, and Bill asked him frantically, "What happened?"

The distraught man stammered a muddled response having to do with, "this girl and I...swimming...undertow..." and Bill began to piece together exactly what had transpired. Lake Ontario is well known for its deep and uncharted undertows. It has claimed the lives of numerous swimmers over the years, many of whose remains have never been recovered to this day.

In the seconds it took for Bill to understand what had happened, he found out that neither the man nor the woman could swim. It was their intention to simply wade into the water, get wet, cool off and then come back out, but the woman had been caught in the strong downward current and had been pulled under. Bill dove into the water and found that he could see very well in front of him thanks to the flashlight which he had stuck down the front of his pants. By a pure stroke of luck, Bill saw her body straight in front of him. She was now face down with her legs and arms extended outward. Bill grabbed her, pulled her in to shore, and the two men lifted her out of the water and placed her limp body gently on the beach.

By now, Mac McDonald and several others had arrived at the scene. Mac was on guard duty when a sailboat out of the Oshawa Yacht Club came sailing close to the beach just off Camp X after having heard the screams for help. Mac yelled out to those on board to stay away and not come any closer to shore, reassuring them that everything was fine. Reluctantly, the occupants of the sailboat continued on their way.

By the time that Lieutenant-Colonel Roper-Caldbeck and Staff Sergeant Maloney got there, Bill and the man were just in the process of pulling the W.A.C. to shore. Out of breath and exhausted, Bill dropped to the ground. Roper-Caldbeck bent over the girl and could see that it was too late.

Bill and another unknown man tried to bring the girl back by alternating giving her mouth to mouth resuscitation. They continued doing this until Doctor Millman arrived. As Millman ran over with bag in hand to where the girl had been placed, Bill Hardcastle asked him hopefully, "Is there anything that we can do for her?"

Doctor Millman pulled a large syringe from his bag and started to fill it. He replied, "I'm afraid not but I'm going to stick her in the heart with this anyway. It will pacify the crowd." After injecting the girl, Millman ordered the men to put her in the back of his car. The doctor then proceeded to Oshawa Hospital where he pronounced her dead.

The women was from Timmons, Ontario. Her mother and father were advised of the accident and her body was shipped back home the next day.

* * *

Captain Howard Benjamin Burgess was sitting in the mess of the prestigious Beaulieu Special Agents Training School in Britain when a Corporal came over to his table and told him that the C.O. would like to see him. Captain Burgess proceeded to the C.O.'s office as requested and knocked on the door.

The C.O. asked him to come in and sit down. He told Burgess that he was needed in Canada as the 'Chief Training Instructor' at a top secret camp. Captain Burgess was elated to hear that he was going to play a major role in 'Secret Warfare'. He could not wait to get there! His C.O. booked him on the next sailing to Canada. Burgess wondered about Canada and what it would be like.

Captain Howard Benjamin Burgess, born August 15, 1915, was a man of only twenty five when he was called upon by his country to perform a very special service. Before the war began, Burgess had worked for the Daily News in London, England, and subsequently was recruited from the Intelligence Training Centre at Matlock where he had served as an N.C.O. (Non Commissioned Officer). His superiors were so impressed with his abilities that they recommended him to the SOE where, on July 23, 1941, he became a Lieutenant Instructor at Beaulieu under Bill Brooker's command.

On April 29, 1942, Howard Benjamin Burgess said goodbye to his mother and father and left Beaulieu for Canada on posting to STS 103 (Camp X). He had been personally requisitioned by Brooker, for whom he had worked on and off since he first joined the Secret Service. Burgess was to replace Major Fairbairn who had previously been "requisitioned" by William Donavon (OSS) from William Stephenson at Camp X to ensure the success of Donavon's new school in Maryland (RTU-11). The BSC and the OSS were known for trading such favours on a regular basis. When Brooker learned that Fairbairn was to be loaned to the OSS, he immediately summoned the bright young man, Burgess, from Beaulieu as Fairbairn's replacement.

Captain Burgess' ship docked at Halifax in late April. As it was his first trip to Canada and because he was urgently needed at Camp X, he was met by a BSC escort, one Herbert Rowland from New York. The two men stayed overnight in a local hotel then boarded a train for Toronto the next morning. The train ride was a grueling sixteen hours, but Captain Burgess enjoyed the scenery of the vast Canadian countryside, something that his young eyes had never seen before.

The two men arrived in Toronto's Union Station and were greeted by a staff car from Camp X. From there they proceeded east on the King's Highway #2 toward Camp X. It was a beautiful spring day and again Captain Burgess enjoyed his ride out through the rich Ontario farmland. He looked eagerly around the Camp as they pulled into the old farm road off Thornton Road. Captain Burgess could not wait to get started for this was exactly what he had dreamed about so often; a chance to make a name for himself.

Captain Burgess settled into Camp routine very nicely and was thoroughly enjoying his new posting as 'Chief Instructor' when catastrophe struck. One day, at the end of May, Burgess was teaching a class of agents how to avoid being stricken by gun fire while crawling through a trench as barbed wire scraped across one's back, when, tragically, a live round caught him in the head. Roper-Caldbeck and Brooker were devastated and could not comprehend how such a thing could have happened.

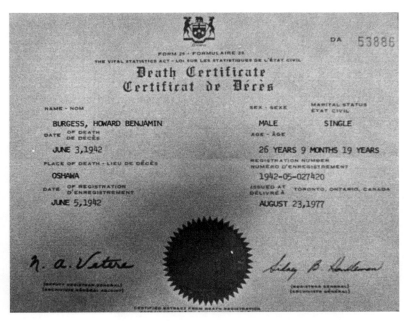

76. *The Death Certificate of Howard Benjamin Burgess*

There was no time to waste. Although Burgess was bleeding profusely from his severe head wound, he was still alive. Dr. Millman was contacted immediately and ordered to meet Roper-Caldbeck and Brooker at the hospital. Camp policy stated that due to the tight security, under no circumstances would emergency services be called into the camp, so Burgess had to be put into the back of a staff car and driven to the Oshawa Hospital.

For five days Burgess fought for his life but finally succumbed to his wounds. His remains were taken to the McIntosh Anderson Funeral Home on King Street in Oshawa and, after preparation, he was buried in the Oshawa Union Cemetery.

The following inscription is on his headstone;

IN PROUD MEMORY OF OUR BELOVED SON
CAPTAIN HOWARD B. BURGESS
INTELLIGENCE CORPS
DIED JUNE 3RD 1942
IN HIS 27TH YEAR

LEST WE FORGET

77. The Grave Stone at Union Cemetery in Oshawa

78. The Burial Permit for Howard Benjamin Burgess

(Authors note: The cause of death was shown to be Acute Glomerular Nephritis, a kidney disease.) His place of residence was listed as simply, "The Sinclair Farm."

Most of the officers and men of Camp X attended the service at the funeral home in Oshawa and took part in the procession afterward. They traveled westward down the old King's Highway # 2, the same route which, just a few weeks earlier, the young Burgess had traveled in the opposite direction toward Camp X, eagerly anticipating his new posting. At the Union

Cemetery, Burgess was laid to rest on a cold and rainy spring day.

At some point during all of these events, a cover-up was instigated. Camp personnel were sworn to secrecy on the matter and the official Camp story was that Burgess had died very suddenly from a cerebral hemorrhage. Stranger still, the 'burial permit' read that he had died from 'acute glomerular nephritis' (a kidney disease).

More on the cover-up of Burgess' death can be found in Chapter X, 'The Investigation of Camp X.'

* * *

Unfortunately, Captain Burgess' accidental death would not be the last at the Camp. Although there was an apparent cover-up relative to this incident, the next death was presented and acknowledged as it had unfolded. Perhaps because, in the case of Burgess, the victim was "one of their's, an SOE British instructor, the whole affair could be taken care of internally. But the next time, the victim was a visiting American and the accident took place in front of witnesses.

In either case, it will most likely never be known why the authorities chose to disclose the following events. As there are no known eye witnesses alive today, the following sequence of events has been recreated from existing bits and pieces of information and is very close to, if not exactly, what happened.

Robert Sherwood, head of the OWI (Office of War Information), was sitting in his office in Manhattan when the phone rang. It was Bill Donavon of the OSS. Bill was excited about the fact that he had just returned from yet another trip to Camp X.

Donavon told Sherwood that he must get up there and see for himself the great things that the BSC and the SOE were doing at their Canadian training school. Sherwood was keenly interested and assured Donovan that he would certainly get on the phone to Brooker right away.

As promised, Sherwood called Brooker and begged him to accommodate some of his own agents for the specialized training which was so badly needed. Brooker said that he would see what he could do and would call him back. That same afternoon, Brooker called Sherwood back and advised him that he had set aside a week for the OWI agents. Sherwood was so enthused about this prospect that he told Brooker he wanted to be there personally to witness the event.

When Sherwood got off the telephone, he called his secretary into the office and asked her to summon Frederick Boissevain, Sherwood's liaison officer, immediately. When Boissevain arrived at Sherwood's office he was told the exciting news and was advised to get packed because the two men would be traveling to Canada together.

79. Frederick Boissevain, OWI

Frederick Boissevain was born in 1903 to a well known Dutch banking family in Amsterdam. He grew up in the Dutch East Indies and in Switzerland, where he studied botany. After working for his father in the family shipping business which allowed him to travel all over the world, he moved to New York and started his career as a horticulturist.

He later moved to Greenwich, Connecticut, where he designed many substantial gardens for clients such as the Rockefeller family. Concurrently, he hosted a weekly gardening radio program and it was during this period that he became a naturalized citizen.

He spoke fluent English, French, German and Dutch making his importance to the future of the OWI obvious given his world travel and the multitude of languages he could speak. Boissevain was determined to be the perfect liaison with Sherwood's OWI special camp on Long Island, New York.

Since Brooker had to divide his attention between Camp X and RTU-11 in Maryland, it was impossible for him to be directly involved with the Long Island school other than to provide occasional assistance. One way in which he was able to help was to assure that the services of Major Skilbeck would be available at a moments notice to travel to Long Island. This agreement worked splendidly and offered the best solution to the needs of the BSC, the SOE, the OSS and the OWI.

On June 23, 1943, Sherwood and Boissevain arrived at Camp X. Sherwood was so impressed with the training that he was most anxious to get a similar program set up at Long Island. This task would be handled by Frederick Boissevain, thus the reason for Boissevain's being brought to the Camp to observe. The two men were witnessing a training exercise when something went tragically wrong. They were watching their own OWI agents in live ammunition exercises firing toward the lake with their Tommy Guns. Even though Frederick Boissevain, as well as the others, was behind protection, he suddenly dropped to the ground, dead. He had been killed instantly.

What apparently happened was a one-in-a-million chance. It is believed by a court of enquiry at the time that two bullets collided in mid air forcing one of the bullets down, accidentally striking Frederick Boissevain in the head. The court of enquiry decided that the cause of Boissevain's demise was "death by misadventure".

Robert Sherwood would accompany his old friend home but hardly in the same joyful spirit in which he arrived.

80. Frederick Boissevain (centre) with other OWI agents

81. The top left hand corner of this aerial photo is where the
protective glass plate was situated. Here, along with Robert Sherwood, Boissevain
watched the training of the OWI agents

Chapter VIII

The Lighter Side of Camp X

Saturday night at Camp X was the night for relaxation. The camp personnel worked hard seven days a week, twelve hours a day, week in and week out. Since Saturday night was party night, most personnel would end up at the mess where the bar was open.

It was on one such Saturday night that two American officers in training as OSS agents each had a little too much to drink and ended the evening by making outrageous and ridiculous bets with each other. After repeatedly wagering as to who could drink the most shots, one agent leaned over and whispered in the other's ear. The recipient of the message yelled out, "You're on!". It was not known until the following day what exactly that final wager was. The two men left the mess arm in arm, weaving toward the Lecture Hall.

The next morning, the two men awoke to splitting headaches. As the self inflicted fog began to clear, one agent began to recall the events of the previous night and reminded the other of the bet made. He was met with a groaned, "Oh, no!" in response.

The two men had a pass for that Sunday and they headed into Oshawa as previously arranged. They went into the Genosha Hotel for breakfast. When they were finished eating, one said to the other, "I'll be back in a moment." Off he went to the washroom and, when he returned, the other could not believe his eyes. They left their table as usual, walked to the counter, paid their bill and went out onto the sidewalk alongside The King's Highway # 2.

There was nothing terribly unusual about their stroll down the street, except for one minor detail; one agent was dressed completely in full German Officer's uniform which they had "liberated" from the lecture hall the previous night! Uniforms of all of the Axis Countries were kept there for identification purposes as part of the agents' training. They walked around town for most of the afternoon without a single person questioning them! The uniformed agent had won his bet!

* * *

On another Saturday night, Mac McDonald and Sergeant Maloney decided that they would love a cold beer, but each had used up his ration coupons for beer at the mess. In a flash of inspiration, Maloney asked Mac, "Why don't we go to the Bowmanville Camp (Camp 30, the German Officer P.O.W. Camp) for a couple of beers?" Mac, recognizing the brilliance of Maloney's idea, was in full agreement!

Maloney knew the Bowmanville Staff Sergeant personally, so when he and Mac arrived at the Camp 30 gate, Maloney asked to see the Staff Sergeant and was escorted in. The two men found that Camp 30 was also on rations, but the men of the Camp did give them a couple of beers each, perhaps in recognition of their ingenuity and audacity.

When it was time for Mac and Sergeant Maloney to leave, they were met and detained by armed guards and had to quickly explain what they were doing there. Maloney said it was his fault as he had convinced the guard to let them in.

Eventually they were able to sort things out and the two men were allowed to leave. Upon their return to Camp X, Maloney and Mac went to Bushell and asked him if he would please intervene as they knew that their escapade had gotten the Camp 30 guard in trouble. Bushell went out to Camp 30 the next day and patched things up with the Commanding Officer.

* * *

One beautiful sunny, afternoon, Bill Hardcastle happened to be walking back to the Hydra building after lunch at the mess hall. Bill was day dreaming, looking at the ground as he passed by the Officer's quarters. That afternoon, as usual, there was a class going on in the field for a group of Yugoslav agents. The class was being conducted by Sergeant-Major de Rewelyskow, the small arms expert.

Out of nowhere Bill heard, "Hey Yorkie!" He looked around but could not see who was calling him. Again he heard, louder, "Hey, Yorkie!" He looked up in the direction the sound seemed to be coming from, and there, on the roof, was de Rewelyskow standing without a stitch of clothes on!

At the end of each graduating class, the students would throw a "shindig" and the trainer would traditionally be the butt of some outlandish prank, much like throwing the coxswain overboard after a race. The class had ganged up on de Rewelyskow and stripped him of his clothes. Somehow, he had ended up on top of the building!

De Rewelyskow yelled, "Just get me down from here, Yorkie, and I'll fetch my sidearm. Then I'll give them a thrill!"

* * *

One day Mac McDonald was on driver duty when he was ordered to go to Union Station in Toronto to pick up an OSS officer. Mac arrived at the appointed time and the officer was there waiting for him.

As soon as the officer got into the car, he asked Mac, "Are you hungry, driver?"

Mac replied, "Sure, I'm always hungry, Sir."

The officer said, "Pull into the King Edward Hotel."

Mac did as the officer said, but was concerned because the OSS officer was dressed in a suit but Mac was only in Canadian Army fatigues. As they walked through the main lobby and then into a very exclusive dining room, the Maitre'd said to Mac, "I am sorry, Sir, but you cannot come in here dressed as you are." Mac said nothing, but the officer immediately pulled the Maitre'd aside and had some words with him.

A few minutes later the Maitre'd walked over to Mac again and said, "I am so sorry, Sir. It seems there has been a misunderstanding. Please, do come in." The officer and Mac walked into the dining room and were seated.

The OSS man asked Mac, "So, what do you feel like having?"

Mac was on a $1.25 'per dieum' expense allowance when on driver duty, and he was aware of the prices at the restaurant they were in, so he replied, "Sir, you order for me please."

The OSS man said, "Well, we're each going to start off with a Filet Mignon steak and... would you like a drink, driver?"

Mac replied, "Yes, Sir, if you're having one."

To which the OSS man said, "Oh, what the hell, driver, we might as well each have a couple of packs of cigarettes on the U. S. Army as well!"

After delivering the OSS officer to the Camp, Mac went straight to Major Bushell and said, "Sir, any time you need anyone to make that run into Toronto, you can count on me!"

* * *

On another occasion, two local fellows were replacing the ground sheet beside Hydra. They were laying a piece of copper about fifteen feet square as a conductor which would give a better ground for the transmitter, and also draw off the static electricity. They seemed to be making a career out of digging the hole and were asking a lot of questions. They asked Bill Hardcastle what the point was of the installation and Bill answered, "I wouldn't ask too many questions if I were you. I'd just dig pretty fast. Sometimes shrapnel from explosives has been known to fly up here."

It was about two or three o'clock in the afternoon and they were still mucking about and smoking on the side of the pit. During lunch, Bill mentioned to Sergeant Court (the explosives expert) that these two fellows were taking a lifetime to dig that hole and were also asking a lot of questions about the Camp. Sergeant Court just smiled and said, "Oh, really. Well, I'll just throw something up there this afternoon to see if we can move things along a bit."

Sergeant Court was instructing a class of French Canadian agents nearby so he was well positioned. An explosion went off shortly after. Bill was near the two diggers when a huge piece of steel came whistling by. A piece of steel flying through the air at high speed has much the same effect as if you were to take a ruler, tie it to a piece of string, and swing it above your head. It was spinning wildly and it sounded like a buzz bomb. It was certainly the biggest piece of red hot flying steel shrapnel these fellows had ever seen or ever hoped to see again. And it was amazing how fast that pit got filled up without another question being asked!

* * *

One day, during the early spring of 1943, Major Bushell called a Private in to his office and said, "Andy, I want you to go down to the mouth of Corbett Creek and clean it out as the ice is backing up." Andy, not too sure exactly how he would accomplish this, stopped off at the mess and asked Mac McDonald if he would help.

Mac asked Andy, "What do they want you to do?"

Andy relied, "Bushell wants me to clear out the ice in the creek."

Mac said, "Sure, Andy, I'll go down with you. It sounds like fun."

The two men jumped in the Jeep and drove to the magazine to get some dynamite. Andy asked Mac, "How much do you think that we'll need?"

Mac replied, "Oh, six sticks ought to do that job."

The two men collected the dynamite and headed down to the lake shore. Andy asked Mac what the method of choice would be in order to get the best results. Mac suggested that they plant the charges six feet apart, starting at the mouth of the creek where it emptied into the lake, and work back up the creek bed from there. They placed the explosives, then set the fuse, got in the Jeep and retreated back about four hundred feet.

As soon as they set off the charge there was a tremendous explosion which sent rocks and ice showering down on the two men in the Jeep. Mac looked down to where the windshield had been previously, in the down position, and noticed that it had been shattered. There was a heavy overcast of cloud cover that day and the percussion from the explosion went outward instead of straight up as it would have done on a clearer day. As Mac would find out later, rocks showered down on the Camp as far back as the Sinclair farmhouse!

Mac and Andy were still sitting in the Jeep when Mac said to Andy, "You just wait. The old man will be down here any minute." Sure enough, not two minutes later a staff car came racing down to the beach.

Bushell jumped out of the car and ran over to the two men who were still sitting in the Jeep. Bushell was so upset that he could hardly get the words out. Stammering wildly, he blurted to the men, "HOW.... MUCH... DID... YOU... USE....?"

Mac replied, "Six sticks, Sir."

Bushell said, still stammering, "SIX...STICKS...!?! Do you know that Major Skilbeck was on the phone with New York and when the charge went off he jumped straight out of his chair!?"

The two men could only reply. "Sorry, Sir."

* * *

Bill Hardcastle received a letter one day ordering him to report to the Ontario Provincial Court in downtown Toronto for jury duty. Bill took the letter to his sergeant, Sergeant Maloney, and asked, "What should I do, Sir?"

Sergeant Maloney replied, "I guess you'll have to go, Bill."

When the day came for Bill to report, he packed his bags not knowing how long he would be there, and a driver took him downtown. As he walked up the steps of the old courthouse building, he was surprised to see Sergeant Maloney standing at the top.

Bill said, "What are you doing here, Sergeant?"

Sergeant Maloney replied, "Give me your papers, Bill, and wait here."

Bill waited for about five minutes and then spotted Maloney walking back out the front door of the courthouse. Sergeant Maloney simply said to Bill, "Let's go back to the Camp now, Bill. It appears they won't be needing you after all."

* * *

Sergeant Court was always looking for things to blow up. One fellow who worked at the Camp had his car freeze up on him one winter. The engine block was frozen solid and the car was rendered useless. Sergeant Court, having heard of the now defunct vehicle, sought out its owner and asked if he might please have it to blow up. The fellow said, "Sure, it's not any good to me any more in that condition. It's all yours." With fiendish glee, Sergeant Court dispatched the useless automobile in a blaze of glory!

* * *

According to Bill Hardcastle, the Camp Commandant had decided that particular spring that the grass just north of the Camp was too tall and dry and was truly a potential fire hazard. The Commandant ordered two instructors to go up and slow burn it. Fortunately for the Camp, there was a thirty foot clear area surrounding the Camp which provided an open area where infiltrators could easily be seen. This area was also near the Jeep patrol.

The two instructors went, as ordered, and started what they thought would be a controlled fire. In no time at all, however, the high winds whipped the fire out of control and sent it blazing toward the Camp itself.

Bill came outside and, looking north toward the fire, could see it getting closer and closer. He said it was the strangest sensation that he had ever experienced; the fire was so intense and the smoke so thick that it sucked the oxygen out of the air even back where he was standing making it impossible to breathe. Bill dropped to the ground where there was a blanket of oxygen and stayed there until the fire hit the open thirty-foot perimeter and burned itself out.

Embarrassment was felt all the way around by the instructors involved.

* * *

On one of those hot and humid Ontario August days, Mac McDonald was guarding the munitions magazine. It had to be guarded twenty four hours a day as it was believed that there were enough explosives stored in the magazine to blow up the entire town of Whitby were there to be an accident or an act of sabotage.

Because it was such a hot and muggy day, and because it was stifling in his full Canadian army uniform, Mac decided to step inside the cool darkness of the magazine to get out of the glaring sun. As usual, Mac had his stogie clenched in his teeth. Although it was not permitted to smoke while on duty, he chewed the unlit cigar out of habit.

Staff Sergeant Maloney was walking by and saw Mac. He was curious as to why Mac would be inside. As he stepped closer, he could see that Mac had a stogie in his mouth. Staff Sergeant Maloney said, "Mac, you wait until Bushell hears about this!," and he ran off to find the Adjutant-Quartermaster.

A few minutes later, Bushell came running down the hill toward the magazine. "Now don't do anything stupid, Mac!," Bushell screamed out. "That thing's not lit, is it?"

"Do you really think that I am that stupid, Sir?" said Mac.

"Mac, you scared the living daylights out of me. Just do me a favour and leave that thing outside when you go inside," said Bushell. Mac did as he was told but could not stop chuckling all afternoon.

82. Mac McDonald plays with his dog while on guard duty

* * *

At the end of his shift guarding the magazine, Mac stopped into the mess to have a cold beer. They were all out of his usual brand and all they had left was a strong ale. Mac said that would have to do as he was very hot and very thirsty. He had one ale and then another. As it was still an hour until his next shift, and because he was drowsy from the heat and the drinks, he decided to go in and have a quick nap. The next thing he knew, he was being shaken by the Sergeant, saying, "Mac, wake up! They're looking for you!"

Mac jumped out of bed, realizing he was late for his guard posting. As he ran out the back way, he could see men walking around looking for him. He managed to time it so he could run over to the magazine and assume his position just as the men came around the building. When they saw him, they said, "Mac, where have you been? We've been looking all over for you!"

Mac casually answered, "I've been here all along. I was just out the back." They were skeptical, but chose not to question him further.

* * *

A few days before Halloween 1943, morale was low among some of the men. They were growing restless with the constant work, week in and week out. They agreed amongst themselves that they had to do something for Halloween to boost their spirits.

They developed a plan of action and took it to Bushell who listened to their proposal and agreed to present it to Lieutenant-Colonel Brooker. The idea was to have a huge Halloween party, complete with female companionship!

Bushell kept to his word and went to see Brooker. The men waited impatiently back in the mess. Finally Bushell came back. "Boys, I've got good news and I've got bad news. The good news is that you can have your party! The bad news is, no women". After all, this was still very serious business.

"No women!?" The guys were devastated. What good would a party be without women? What about morale? But it was obvious that the decision was final. There would be no negotiating. They would just have to make the best with what they had. The men reluctantly agreed, "Fine, if we can't have women, we'll just have to make our own."

The men had their party, and they had a great time. And their "women" were perfectly stunning! The pictures below will attest to that!

83. The lovely ladies of Camp X, Halloween, 1943

* * *

One particular Saturday night, Bill Hardcastle and Eric Adams had gone into town for some rest and relaxation. They soon found a "watering hole" and settled in for the evening.

84. Bill Hardcastle celebrates on V.E. Day

Sergeant-Major de Rewelyskow had had a long, tough day training a group of American trainees and had decided to settle into bed early. Meanwhile, Bill and Eric were well on there way to getting 'tight', as they would say. They returned to the Camp late that night and decided to have some fun. They sneaked along behind the Officer's Quarters until they got to de Rewelyskow's room, where they started to pick up some pebbles and lightly toss them at his window. After a while they grew bored with this, so they headed off to their rooms for the night.

At breakfast, Bill and Eric were sitting at one of the tables when de Rewelyskow came in and sat down near them. He said, "Did we have a good time last night, lads?" Then he got up and walked over to Eric and yelled, "I know that you were one of them, Eric, weren't you?" and he drove his erect and straightened fingers directly into Eric's stomach. As Eric doubled over in pain, Bill sensed what was going to happen next and took a glass ashtray off the table and stuck it down his pants. De Rewelyskow walked around to where Bill was sitting and jabbed Bill in the stomach in the same manner. He quickly brought his hand up, holding it in pain and muttering, "I'll get you for this Bill!", as he walked away.

And get Bill he did! A few days later de Rewelyskow was conducting a class of agents in unarmed combat when he said to the group, "Now, I need a volunteer. Corporal, go fetch Yorkie and tell him I don't care what he's doing, drop everything and get down here."

Bill, upon hearing the news that he was wanted right away by de Rewelyskow, thought to himself, "Oh no, he's going to get me now." He walked as slowly as possible along the roadway toward the large barn where the training was taking place. When he got there, he could see de Rewelyskow and the agents patiently waiting for him. "You wanted to see me, Sir?," asked Bill.

"Yes, Bill. Be a good chap and come over here while I show these lads a few things," replied de Rewelyskow.

The next thing Bill knew he was twirling around in the air like a toy airplane! And, from that moment on, every time that de Rewelyskow reached this point in his training program, the words would ring out, "Corporal, go fetch Yorkie."

* * *

Once, during some aggressive training in the old barn, one of the instructors got carried away in his zealous obsession with realism. While working with live ammunition, he accidentally caused a spark igniting the dry grass surrounding the building.

All hell broke lose as the wind swept the grass fire directly toward the magazine where the explosives were stored. Andy Daniels was one of the agents being trained that day and remembered it well.

85. The grass fire burns dangerously close to the explosives magazine at the far left of the photograph

"We created a human chain of men with every available bucket we could find. The line stretched from the magazine back to the old Sinclair farmhouse where the artesian well was. For a time, all of us were extremely concerned about whether or not we were going to be able to get the fire out before it hit the magazine." In the end, they were successful as can be attested to by the fact that Andy was able to tell the story some thirty years later.

* * *

Mac McDonald was on guard duty at the front gate one day when Sergeant Paterson walked up to him and said, "Brigadier-General Volk is coming in today to meet with Brooker. You keep your eyes open and tell me just as soon as you see him approaching." Mac kept a close vigil on the old farm road looking eastward towards Thornton Road.

After an hour or more, Mac saw in the distance the convoy of three cars, each with flags waving on either side. They turned off Thornton Road, followed along the old farm road and were heading straight toward him. He got on the telephone right away.

"Sergeant Paterson, Sir, the convoy has just arrived", said Mac.

Sergeant Paterson replied, "Mac, don't lift that gate until I tell you to; I'll be right there."

The convoy stopped at the gate just as Sergeant Paterson arrived. He leaned into the car and asked, "May I see your identification, Sir?"

The Brigadier-General fumbled through his clothes and said, "I don't believe that I have any with me. I have only this pay slip with my name on it."

Sergeant Paterson looked at it. "That will be fine, Sir, but I'll just ride along on the running board with you to make sure that you proceed through the Camp without incident."

He ordered Mac to get on the telephone and let Major Brooker know that the Brigadier-General had arrived. When the vehicle reached the Commanding Officer's residence, Sergeant Paterson announced the arrival of the Brigadier-General. As soon as the Brigadier-General was safe inside, Sergeant Paterson ran back to the guard house to complete his own "mission". Out of breath, he said, "Mac, guess what? The Brigadier-General makes $10,000 a month!" Mac broke up with laughter at the Sergeant's antics.

Chapter IX

The Bowmanville Connection (Camp 30)

The Bowmanville connection to Camp X was extraordinary, to say the least. Unless you belonged to the Axis Group and you were in a German occupied country, there was nowhere else on earth, other than at Camp X, where you could summon a German officer and have him sitting in your office within a half hour. Located only minutes away from Camp X, in Bowmanville, Ontario, was a German Officer's Internment Camp during the Second World War, officially known as Camp 30.

One of the buildings of Camp X referred to earlier, the Lecture Hall, was used for training agents using black board theory and also housed artifacts of German weaponry, uniforms and insignia, all confiscated from the captive officers in detention at Camp 30. The admonishment above the door, "Know Your Enemy," was not taken lightly; herein was conducted the most detailed training in exactly that aspect of the secret war.

Early on in the war, it became evident to the British that they had to establish a detention centre for German prisoners of war, especially officers. They needed to find a location that would be safe, still in a Commonwealth country, but as far from Britain as possible. Camp 30 satisfied all these criteria. The British could not afford to take their captured German officers back to Britain for, in the event that Germany were to be successful in invading Britain, the German Officers would then have been released immediately and put back into battle from within Britain. Therefore, they sent their captured German officers to Canada where, ironically, they ended up incarcerated only thirty minutes from Camp X.

86. The German officers' POW Camp 30, under construction

This was a major advantage for the Commandant of Camp X who could call upon his counterpart at the Bowmanville Camp 30 and request that a German officer be sent to him for "special work". The German officer would be ordered to interrogate the agents-in-training in exactly the same manner which he would use were he to capture a British agent back in Germany.

The British agent would be put through the same rigorous interrogation, save torture. All of this was explained in advance to the agent in great detail so that there would be no misunderstanding of what could happen to him were the Nazis not satisfied with his responses.

The agent would then be stripped of his clothes in order to demoralize him, placed in a specialized chair with a hole in the seat, and an uncomfortably bright light would be shone directly in his eyes.

87. A German POW, typical of the Interragators brought from Camp 30

As the interrogator (an English-speaking German officer from Bowmanville) slowly formulated his questions, the agent had to remain completely immobile; if he moved his head up, he would receive an electrical shock from a charged plate placed just above him. If he tried to relax, his buttocks would be jabbed with spikes situated just below the hole in the chair seat. This training would indeed later prove to be invaluable to Andy Daniels when he was captured by the Hungarian counter intelligence officers, and undoubtedly saved him undue discomfort when he was subsequently put through exactly the same procedures.

The SOE ordered that the agent hold out for forty eight hours at any cost. After that, the agent was to divulge only what he felt he must. This, of course, was designed as a stalling tactic to give the other agents in the local circuit time to move out and eliminate any trace of their existence.

* * *

The German POW camp, Camp 30, was built originally as a boys reformatory in 1925 by the Ontario Government. It was designated as an area where delinquent juveniles could benefit from being placed in an open country environment yet still maintain the discipline that was found at more conventional penal establishments. The school functioned very well as a reformatory during the years from 1925 to 1941. Throughout those same years, more buildings were added to the complex. A gymnasium, a swimming pool and other recreational buildings were all designed and constructed to make the boys' stay there as comfortable as possible.

88. A group of German officer POW's at Camp 30

With the British concerns for the invasion of Britain in 1940, the Canadian Government was approached with the request that a camp facility be made available for the purpose of detaining captured German officer POW's. The Canadian Government quickly concurred. It made sense to establish the camp in Bowmanville because of its proximity to so many military establishments in and around the Toronto area such as the Canadian Army headquarters at Military District No. 2 in downtown Toronto, and the over twenty thousand soldiers housed in what was then, and still remains, the Horse Palace at the Canadian National Exhibition Grounds, also in Toronto. In the event of an emergency, soldiers could be at Camp 30 within an hour. Even given the close proximity to Toronto, Bowmanville was still far enough away that it was in the country and remote enough that it would not be seen by the general public.

It took only the span of a weekend for word to come down from Ottawa that the Bowmanville site was satisfactory and was to be converted immediately into a POW camp. The boys currently residing at the school were to be taken to other temporary locations immediately in and around the Bowmanville area.

89. During the battle of Britain, a Spitfire takes aim at Priebe's Messerschmidt. There is no time to take corrective measures

While Ottawa was scurrying around making the necessary arrangements for Camp 30, hundreds of miles away and across the sea, Eckehart Priebe was heavily involved in a dogfight with a group of Spitfires over England at the height of the "Battle of Britain." Priebe had his thumb on the red firing button of his powerful Messerschmidt airplane. His sites were clearly aimed at the Spitfire straight ahead of him. As the Spitfire darted back and forth trying to evade the Messerschmidt, Priebe instinctively determined when the time was right to fire.

90. As the Spitfire bears down on the Messerschmidt,
Pribe's life is about to change dramatically

Priebe fired his guns. Nothing happened. He fired again, and still
nothing. Glancing back, he noticed a couple of Spitfires on his tail. Before
he had time to react, the glass of his canopy shattered and he felt a searing
pain through his head. As he saw his own blood spatter on the broken
canopy, he realized that he had been hit and was going down. He quickly
ejected, his parachute opened, and the ground came racing up to meet him.
As Priebe looked down, he could see the waiting guards with rifles aimed at
him. This was it for Priebe. There was no escape.

After some recovery time in an English hospital, Eckehart Priebe was
put on a ship heading across the Atlantic and, unbeknownst to him, to Camp
30. Priebe would serve the next six years at the Camp.

By the summer of 1941, the decision had already been made to convert
Bowmanville. It became readily apparent that additional barracks would
need to be erected in order to house the anticipated number of officers that
would be in residence there. The German POW's were transported to Canada
via ship using the North Atlantic Supply Route, the logic being that if one of
the German U-boats were to sink one of the British supply ships making the
voyage across the treacherous waters, that the concurrent drowning of a
number of German officers would help to compensate for the loss. By the
time the first group of German officers were en route to Canada as prisoners
of war, the construction of additional barracks was well under way and
would be completed in a few short weeks.

It is difficult to understand why any of the German officers would want
to escape the beautiful confines of Camp 30, with all of its amenities within,
to return to Germany and the horrors of the front lines. In point of fact,
numerous attempts to escape were made, usually by tunneling out of the
Camp, occasionally successfully.

As the war years continued and things got progressively worse for the
Germans, the number of POW's at Camp 30 swelled to over six hundred.
The meals served by the numerous kitchens were sectioned off by rank, just
as they were in any military camp or compound, and were of the best

quality food that could be found during the war years. Portions were generous and there were numerous selections available. Much of the food was home grown by the POW's on the large farm adjacent to the camp. They grew vegetables, kept cows for fresh dairy products, and raised other farm animals for meat.

It is certainly noteworthy that, after the war, many of the German officers who were released and sent home to Germany chose to return to Canada with their families and indeed ended up living not very far from Camp 30. One such officer, Otto Kretschmer, had been the Commander of the German U-boat, U-99. Kretschmer had been the most successful of all of the U-boat Commanders at sinking Allied ships and was personally congratulated by Adolf Hitler himself. Before his capture, Kretschmer, had sunk forty four ships for a total of 266,629 tons of supplies which were headed toward the Allied troops through the North Atlantic Supply Route.

Many articles have been written over the years describing eye-witness accounts of U-boats having been spotted in the St. Lawrence River. The obvious question is, of course, why German U-boats would be sent as far up river as Maisonette Point at the Bay of Chandler. The reason is now evident. An elaborate plan had been devised to smuggle key POW's out of Camp 30, rendezvous with the U-boats on the St. Lawrence, and return the rescued officers to Germany to be reinstated them back into the war as quickly as possible.

Such was the case with Otto Kretschmer. Admiral Karl Donitz wanted Kretschmer back in the "Wolf Pack". He was able to get a message to Kretschmer advising him that a U-boat would pick him up at a designated time and place. All Kretschmer had to do was get out of Camp 30.

Dontiz had devised a plan and, through his agents in Canada, was able to smuggle Canadian money, forged documents, topographical maps, train schedules, highway maps and maps of Canada's east coast into Camp 30. The POW's devised an elaborate system of tunnels under Camp 30, much like those depicted in the movies made over the years. The prisoners were ingenious in creating various schemes for escape, making shovels out of tin cans, storing soil in the cuffs of their pants to be raked back into the ground as it was released from their pant cuffs, and even storing the soil in the ceilings of the buildings.

91. The Officers Quarters in the Triple Dorm Building where, on 31 August, 1943, the Canadian Camp 30 personnel found the largest of the tunnels in the northeast corner of the building shortly before the German POW's would have broken through and escaped

It was through one of these tunnels that Kretschmer would have made his escape and effected the rendezvous with the German U-boat were it not for the love of a garden by one of his fellow German POWs. Kretschmer sat waiting in the tunnel for the right time to make his break. All he could think about was the German U-boat that was cruising toward Canada on a destination to pick him up. Then, moments before Kretschmer was to surface and make his getaway, another POW, not aware of the tunnel, went out into the back grounds behind his quarters in search of some top soil for his flower bed. The man was digging while talking with some friends. When his shovel broke through the soil, he suddenly found himself shoulder deep in the ground.

The prisoner had broken through into the tunnel and the caper was over for Kretschmer. He would spend the next twenty eight days in solitary confinement and the remaining war years at Camp 30.

* * *

Certainly worth mentioning at this point is the famous Battle of Bowmanville. Approximately six hundred POW's barricaded themselves in their barracks for three days, refusing to follow orders. So began the long standoff between the POW's and the Camp guards who were supported by additional army personnel brought in from the outside.

After three days, and the influx of over five hundred elite Canadian troops, the German POW's barracks were eventually stormed and order was restored by shackling the German officers. In the days after the battle, routines were gradually re-established and life at the Camp returned to normal.

* * *

The following story, by Ron Lowman, appeared in the Toronto Star on

February 25, 1979, and offers a good insight into what was going on at Bowmanville. This article is, "Reprinted with permission — Toronto Star Syndicate".

"It's infuriating any time a journalist gets scooped on a good yarn, but when it happens 37 years after the event, what can you say?

92. Gerneral Johann Von Ravenstein escaped an assassination attempt by barricading himself in his room

"Ravenstein; Portrait of a German General, (published in Canada by Thomas Nelson and Sons, 214 pages), a book by British author Rowland Ryder, unveils an inside story of the 1942 Battle of Bowmanville between German prisoners-of-war and Canadian camp guards, which The Star was prevented from publishing by wartime Ottawa censors. It also tells some unreported stories about a secret kangaroo court convened in the Bowmanville camp by angry U-boat commanders to try a fellow-prisoner for surrendering his boat, and an assassination attempt on General Johann von Ravenstein by two fanatical Nazi SS (Schutzstaffel) officers.

"The pair decided his enthusiasm for the Nazi (as distinct from the German) cause was tepid and held their own summary court martial, at which von Ravenstein wasn't present, and passed a death sentence.

"Friends warned the general, who barricaded his room with furniture and foiled the SS men's efforts to break in. Next morning, van Ravenstein was transferred to the camp hospital with a minor heart attack and the SS officers were dispatched to another prison camp.

"Ryder, the author, gathered his material on the Bowmanville camp from Friedrich von Goetz of Toronto, after being introduced to him by mail by Ron Lowman. Lowman never met Ryder, who obtained Lowman's name from British sources.

"Lowman had been in the Commonwealth Air Training Plan at the time of the Bowmanville battle but knew nothing of what was going on there.

"Von Goetz, a former Luftwaffe pilot and a Canadian now for many years, knew von Ravenstein well as his senior officer at Bowmanville, which housed pilots, the U-boat men and Afrika Korps officers.

"Von Ravenstein, an officer and gentleman of the old Prussian Junker tradition, had been a page to the Kaiser Wilhelm and for remarkable gallantry in World War I had been awarded the Pour le Merite (the Blue Max), Germany's highest decoration of that era.

"A tank general in World War II in the Western Desert, he was captured, torpedoed by his own side, spent months as a prisoner in Cairo, Alexandria and South America and had a hand in an attempt by one thousand German POWs to seize the ship SS Pasteur en route to Durban.

"Later, at Bowmanville, van Ravenstein prevented the kangaroo court from trying the U-boat commander and politely refused a request by the camp commandant, a Colonel Bull, to have one hundred men shackled as retaliation of Allied POW's. That is when the Battle of Bowmanville began.

"Regular Canadian troops were dispatched to reinforce the Veteran's Guard and Ryder reports that eventually the fighting became a good-natured affair, with the Canadian soldiers throwing aside their bayonets. One hundred Germans were handcuffed, but in a week it was all forgotten.

"Gwyn 'Jocko' Thomas, who worked for the Toronto Star, remembers the battle well. The Star covered it exclusively after receiving an inside tip. Seven staffers under the late Major Claud Pascoe, OBE (Order of the British Empire), a veteran of the Crimea and World War I, rented a whole floor in a local hotel and went to work piecing the story together.

" 'I remember crawling through an apple orchard near the prison camp and being warned by a guard with a fixed bayonet to get out, or else' Thomas said.

" 'We filed stories and pictures to the Star for four days, but the censor, Bert Perry, had his orders from Ottawa and nothing was published. It was frustrating as hell'.

93. Officers' mess, scene of the "Battle of Bowmanville"

"Thomas recalled a number of POW escapes from camps at Gravenhurst, Bowmanville and Monteith. On one, Thomas and Toronto Telegram reporter Perc Cole tried to get into the main gate of the Gravenhurst camp, but were bounced. Cole then phoned his city editor, Bert Wemp, a World War I major in the Royal Flying Corps, and told him to send a wire to Cole reading; 'Report to Colonel Bull (Camp Commandant) at once. Signed Major Wemp.'

"They waved the wire at the Veterans' Guard and got in. Two minutes later, with the irate Bull threatening to arrest them, they came hurtling out again in their car.

"Thomas said it was tough covering POWs and incidents in their camps because the military wouldn't co-operate. 'They were scared of reprisals in Germany against Canadian POWs if stories appeared', Thomas said. 'It was something to do with the Geneva convention, too.'

"Eventually, after a number of escapes, the military sought the help of newspapers in running pictures of prisoners who were on the loose.

"Thomas remembers the late Norman Phillips of the Star driving home from Espanola and picking up a suspicious character who was hitch-hiking. Convinced he was an escaped German, Phillips dropped him at Huntsville with the excuse that he had to see someone, but would pick him up again on the south edge of town if he hadn't got a lift.

"Phillips drove on into Huntsville, heard a band, spotted a military church parade and pleaded with the officer in charge to come and grab the man.

" 'You're drunk. Get off the road,' Phillips was told. Finally, he ran to the police station to Chief W. C. Carson and together they arrested the German on Highway 11.

"Photographer Strathy 'Stogie' Smith, sent to the scene with Jocko Thomas, was shooting pictures like mad when the army appeared and threatened to arrest him if he didn't give up his film.

" 'Strathy tossed the film holder to me. I caught the forward pass and ran like hell,' Thomas said. 'We got the film back to Toronto.' "

The Battle of Bowmanville was the last significant incident to take place at Camp 30, with the exception of those relative to the ties to Camp X as mentioned previously.

94. POW barracks at Camp 30 as they are in February 1999

Chapter X

The Investigation of Camp X

It was a beautiful sunny, warm, afternoon in July of 1977. Marlene, my wife, and I, the author of *Inside-Camp X*, were enjoying our new home on Shannon Court in Whitby, Ontario. Marlene was in her hammock reading and I was lying in a lounge chair just taking in the sun. I had my head back, my eyes closed and was thinking about absolutely nothing. I had been working hard at my job installing a new computer system and the long drive and long hours were taking their toll on me. I was enjoying this Sunday afternoon and nothing was going to get me out of this chair.

That was until Marlene said, "I'll bet that's near here!" Those spoken words were about to change my life in a big way...

"What's near here?" I asked.

She said, "Camp X. There was a training ground somewhere near Whitby. From the way it's described, it must be near by."

It took me back to 1964 when Mar and I were first married. We often went to a local movie theater. The movie that was showing at the Elgin Theatre one particular evening was one of Ian Fleming's "James Bond" movies. It went into great detail about the training of the SOE agents, although they were not called "SOE" agents at that time, and it peaked my interest.

I remember coming out of the theatre thinking, " I'm sure there was a training camp somewhere in the Toronto area." There was no information available then, and we went home and thought little more about it until that day in the back yard twelve years later.

I got out of my lounge chair, walked into the house, got dressed and said to Marlene, " I'm going to go look around". I went to downtown Whitby and started to ask questions of the older people who worked in the stores and who had lived in town during the war.

Someone said, "Oh yeah. It was down at the lake." He thought if you went down Thornton Road, it would take you right to where the camp had been.

I went home and told Mar that I had found someone who knew about the Camp and even thought he knew where it might have been. Again, not knowing exactly where to look, I let it go at that point. A few days later, at work, I was thinking to myself that perhaps, if I were to drive down to the area and knock on some doors, someone would remember something about the Camp. It was on a Tuesday evening and it was summer so it did not get dark until 9:00 or 9:30 p.m.

I started out down Thickson Road. There were a number of cottages that had been there during the war and which were now general housing. I stopped at one house and no one was home. I went next door and was told that yes, there was someone who lived around here who was involved with the Camp during the Second World War and was directed to his home. I continued down the road past a few more houses, pulled into the designated driveway and knocked on the door. An older gentleman, about sixty five years of age, came to the door and I told him that I was looking for someone who had worked at Camp X during World War II.

A big smile spread across his face as he said, "Well, you've found him. I worked there during the second World War." From there began my friendship with Bill Hardcastle.

Bill invited me in and I told him of my interest in Camp X. Right from the start Bill was very secretive and evasive and would not tell me anything about exactly when he was there, what he did there, or what was going on at the Camp. Nothing specific at all. But it was a beginning.

I asked him if I were to come back and present him with some credentials attesting to my attempt to create a museum for Camp X, would he then co-operate with me. On those terms he agreed to an interview.

I returned to Bill's home several times over that summer. After a period of time, Bill told me exactly where the camp had been located and gave me directions how to get there. It was just a stone's throw from where he lived. I was able to find the Camp and eventually had him come with me to verify locations. This was difficult at first for Bill. He was, as I said, a secretive man and he had taken an oath of silence with the BSC during World War II. It was a life long oath which he took very seriously and it was not easy getting any information out of Bill Hardcastle.

Eventually, I discovered the key to Bill's trust. I thought, Bill likes tomato sandwiches, toasted tomato sandwiches. I will take him one of my tomato plants. I put one of the plants in a pot, put a stake in it and headed over to Bill's place. He opened the door and his big smile appeared once again. He asked, "What's this?"

I said, "It's a tomato plant for you. You can watch it grow and when the tomatoes are big and ripe you can have a nice fresh tomato sandwich." Bill just thought that was great. He took it right out to the patio and put it on the table beside his chair in the sun. We went inside, sat down and talked some more about different things relative to the Camp.

The next time I went over to Bill's, a Saturday as I recall, I knocked on the door. When no one answered, I went around to the back and there was Bill, sitting in his chair, staring at his tomato plant. Watching the tomatoes ripen.

I asked, "What are you doing"?

Bill said, "Oh, just watching my plant".

"That's good. Everything O.K.?", I asked.

" Oh yeah, it's just coming along fine. The tomatoes are getting bigger. You know, I don't leave it outside. When I go in, I take the plant in with me and every morning I bring it back outside. Some cats around here have been after it and there are some kids down the street that have been looking at it. I don't take any chances with it so I bring it in the house."

From that point on, I was his good friend. We would sit for hours talking about Camp X. Little by little he began to tell me what went on there and what his role had been. Bill was an invaluable source of information.

Once I actually got to the site, it gave me a very eerie feeling. I walked along the roads that once linked all the buildings which were long since gone. They had been destroyed years ago and only the foundation of each remained. Even knowing what little I did at that time about what had transpired there, where so many agents had completed their training, I found the Camp filled with ghostly echoes.

Walking from one end to the other, north to south, was quite a long walk. It took a good ten minutes. As I walked down to the lake, it was very easy to imagine where various things had taken place. There were huge craters left where the explosives had been tested, very large holes three or four feet deep and about ten to twenty feet in diameter. When I got to the lake, I took my shoes and socks off, rolled up my pants and began to walk along the shoreline. The water was clear and I could see the bottom. I was able to pull things out of the water; knives, spoons and even plates. There were also many large chunks of metal shrapnel, the remains of the explosives which had landed on the beach and in the water.

During that summer of 1977, I visited Bill Hardcastle almost daily. Just a short time after the tomato plant episode, on one such visit, I found Bill to be quiet and very reserved. After much coaxing, he disclosed to me that he had just had a visit from the RCMP reminding him that he had taken an oath of secrecy for life. I asked him how they had known that he had been talking with me and he indicated that he had no idea. The corporal who had visited simply reminded him of his oath, then got in his car and drove away.

* * *

Early on in my investigation, I began to notice an odd occurrence. At the end of a telephone conversation regarding Camp X, there would be a peculiar noise after the other person had hung up. I would listen a bit longer and then I would hear a "click". Mostly as a joke, and never really believing that there was someone on the line, I would sometimes say something like, " Well guys, I hope you got all of that." Or, "Sorry about the fact that there wasn't much information. Better luck next time."

Not long after this, I got a phone call from a corporal in the RCMP. He said he would like to have a meeting with me and we agreed on a location. Ironically, it was the Genosha Hotel where a lot of the Camp X meetings had taken place many years before.

We agreed to meet one Saturday morning for breakfast. He explained to me that some of things I was doing were covered by the Official Secrets Act, and that if I continued with my investigation, I could be charged. Not knowing my legal limitations, I asked him, "What kind of arrangements can we make?"

He told me that if I were to bring all of my findings to him, and if they did not violate the Official Secrets Act, then I could use them in my work. At that time, Alan Longfield and I, my wife Marlene, and Alan's wife Judi, were publishing the Camp X Museum Society Journal called "25-1-1".

From that time forward, the RCMP Corporal and I had a standing arrangement that we would meet every third Saturday at the Genosha Hotel for breakfast and I would bring to him any new information I had discovered. He would then review it and say "Yea" or "Nay". In one edition of the Journal, we had wanted to run the Igor Gouzenko story but that was turned down at that time by the RCMP Corporal as still being classified information.

There were other stories which were deemed "Classified" by the RCMP and that I was not allowed to publish. The Howard Benjamin Burgess story was one, for example. I could not investigate any such classified information beyond what I had already discovered and I agreed to comply with what could or could not be published in the journal. In spite of the occasional frustration, the arrangement worked out well in the end.

* * *

Two years after the SOE had moved out of the Camp, and while it was still in the hands of the BSC, Camp X was thrown into the middle of an international political intrigue. A young Russian cipher clerk was stationed at the Russian Embassy in Ottawa. One afternoon, the young man got up from his desk, picked up his brief case and walked out the door. After walking a few blocks, the man turned into the entrance way to a Canadian Federal building, went through the front doors and asked to see the person in charge.

Igor Gouzenko had had enough of spying for Russia in Canada and asked for political asylum. The Canadian Government had never experienced anything like this before and did not know what the protocol was in these circumstances. They detained Gouzenko in a room, questioning him repeatedly and extensively regarding his information and his intentions. Meanwhile, frantic phone calls were made throughout the capital of Ottawa.

After numerous calls, the officials finally found someone who seemed to know how to handle the situation. A phone call was then placed to William Stephenson and that night, after making some additional phone calls of his own, Stephenson arrived at the door of the hotel room where Igor Gouzenko was being detained. The man to whom Stephenson had spoken also made his appearance shortly thereafter.

Later that same evening, Gouzenko and his family were taken from Ottawa and transported to Camp X where they would remain throughout the Royal Commission Inquiry that was mandated to look into the allegations regarding his activities.

95. Igor Gouzenko (left) and an RCMP agent outside the Bravener House

Igor Gouzenko had in his possession a briefcase which contained confidential documents outlining the depth of the Russian spy network that was active in Canada and the United States at that time. It is amazing given the level of skill and the capability of the Russian intelligence service that, to the best of our knowledge, during the entire time that Igor Gouzenko was under protection of the Canadian Government at Camp X, the Russians had absolutely no knowledge of his whereabouts.

Even had the Russians been able to ascertain that Gouzenko was at Camp X, in fact he really was not in the Camp at all. Many people who served at the Camp for the duration of the war stated that they had never seen him there. That is true, they did not and with good reason. The old Sinclair house, by 1945, was in rough shape. The agents had taken a toll on it and it was not fit for occupation. Stephenson acquired another farmhouse which was in excellent condition and only a very short distance from the Camp and this became the Gouzenko residence.

This "new" old farmhouse, known as the Bravener House, was at the bottom of Thornton Road, with the lake for a front yard. It was ideally situated just south of the entrance to the Camp, where it could easily be protected by either the Camp personnel or the RCMP, yet was far enough away that it would not create suspicion. Those working inside Camp X would virtually never see the Gouzenko family.

* * *

Camp X lives on today in a very strange way. During the late seventies, I was told that one of the buildings had been preserved and "recycled." I met a man through mutual acquaintances who had been invited, at the time of the Camp's demolition, to help himself to whatever artifacts he wanted.

This man had been so impressed with the materials that had been used to build the Camp that he renovated his entire recreation room in his home with them. When I went to visit him to view these artifacts, I came to learn that there was still one existing building. When the order had been given for the Camp to be destroyed, the town of Whitby amazingly allowed private citizens the opportunity to take the buildings, intact, for whatever purpose they wished, the only provision being that the new owner assume the responsibility for all moving costs. A Muriel Sissons bought the agents' barracks for the grand sum of one dollar and then donated it to the Whitby Humane Society on Thickson Road for use as an animal clinic.

96. The only remaining building belonging to Camp X, the agents barracks, is currently owned by the Whitby Humane Society

One day after work, Alan Longfield and I drove to the Whitby Humane Society in search of the agents' barracks. We pulled into the driveway on Thickson Road and there it was, right in front of us. It looked exactly as it had during the war. Nothing had been changed on the outside, but the interior had been stripped in preparation for turning it into a dog kennel. The dark-shingled roof and the exterior white asbestos tiles were completely intact.

It had been our hope at that time to re-secure the building with the intention of converting it into a museum, but that plan had to be abandoned because of insufficient funds. The building still exists today as a living memory of Camp X, the only original building in existence, some sixty years later.

* * *

After discovering the cover-up involving Howard Benjamin Burgess' death, I decided to take a copy of his death certificate to a doctor, thirty five years after the fact. After examining the document, she told me that this person had died from kidney disease and had suffered for a long time from the disease prior to his death. She further stated that someone suffering from this diagnosis would have been very weak and extremely sick. Obviously not the strong, young, healthy man that was Burgess!

So why was this cause of death shown on the official certificate? No one will ever know now, as all of those who were witnesses at the time are deceased. Back in 1977, however, I learned of one witness who was still working at the funeral home and I decided to see if it would be possible for me to interview him. I parked outside the funeral home, walked in the front door, and asked for the gentleman by name. Shortly thereafter a man came out to greet me and pleasantly said, "I'm Mr. ..., how may I help you?"

I said, "I'm investigating the death of a Howard Benjamin Burgess who was killed at Camp X during the Second World War."

The man's face turned white, his entire demeanor changed, and he said, "I have no comment." I tried to press him further but he just became more agitated.

I asked him why the death certificate said that Burgess had died from kidney failure when in fact he had died from a gun shot wound to the head. At this point, the attendant said that he would have to ask me to leave, and that I was not to come back again.

I received the true story regarding Burgess' demise from an eye witness confidant. Even the Foreign and Commonwealth Office in London, England, when I wrote them regarding the mysterious death, stated, "Unfortunately he sustained a cerebral hemorrhage during the night of May 28, 1942 and died on June 3, 1942 in hospital", signed E. G. Boxshall.

* * *

Later on, toward the end of the seventies, I had a falling out with one of the other members of the Camp X Museum Society. It had been my intention to build a simple museum from the only existing original building that remained at the time. The museum would be placed on the original site of the Camp and would be protected by the same security firm that would guard the new Ontario Liquor Control Board warehouse which subsequently occupied a good part of the Camp X site.

Thus, we would have had a museum which would have been the original agents' barracks on the site of Camp X, filled with Camp X artifacts and memorabilia. But this was not to be. Other members of the Society wanted something more impressive. They had grandiose ideas of building a miniature village with all of the original buildings replicated complete with a church, shopping malls, hotels and so forth. My small, practical plan for a memorial museum costing a few thousand dollars to construct, had mushroomed to an estimated SIX MILLION DOLLAR project!

I was almost ready to step aside and abandon my dream at this point, but one of our members of the Camp X Museum Society, Alan Dewar, a local Oshawa Councilor, was summoned to speak to the executive of the Oshawa based United Auto Workers Union (U.A.W.). They apparently were upset about the reconstruction of Camp X and wanted to hear a "justification for our actions."

I asked Alan, "You're not going to go are you?"

He said, "Yes, I have to. I'm a Councilor."

"We don't have to justify our project to these people as it has nothing to do with them!"

"I have my reasons why I need to go. I can't refuse."

To which I said, "All you will do is fuel their fire for their own agenda."

And that is exactly what happened. Alan Dewar went to the U.A.W. Oshawa Hall and appeared before their combined Executive and general membership. It did not take long for the booing and shouting to start as Alan was pummeled with question after question. One man, originally from Britain, stood up and said, "We'll not have this money wasted on this stupid idea when we need better benefits and higher wages!" That was it for me. I could see that this was going nowhere quickly. Little did the U.A.W. care about the fact that, had the plan been approved and implemented, it would have created hundreds of jobs in the community both in the trades and for on-going tourism.

The next day, the U.A.W. story hit the local papers with a negative blast not felt since the last charge was set off at Camp X in 1944. Immediately after reading the article, one Councilor after another, all once one hundred percent behind the project, dropped their support for Camp X.

It was shortly after the U.A.W. debacle that the entire project collapsed, the Ontario Liquor Control Board warehouse was built, and a simple monument to Camp X was erected on the site.

Now, all of these years later, I have renewed my personal commitment to see the project completed.

* * *

To this day, the intriguing methods of the SOE continue. One day, while working on this book, I clicked onto my Camp X web site in order to check my guest book (http://webhome.idirect.com/~lhodgson/campx.htm) and I found that I had a new entry from a man in the United States. It simply said, "Please provide a safe e-mail address".

I did just that by replying to his e-mail with just one line, 'lhodgson@idirect.com'. The next day, I checked my e-mail and again found that I had a message waiting from this same individual. His e-mail said that he had a special interest in Camp X as his father had been there. That was the entire message. I was, of course, very interested as I was still compiling the research for this book. I sent back a message asking him some specific questions about his father. Was he still alive? What branch was he with? To my dismay, I did not receive any reply.

I started to research the man's name and determined exactly why my last contact had been met with silence. The first message sent to me had been a test to find out how much I already knew. My answer was not satisfactory in that I had not recognized the name of my contact.

As it turns out, the man who had e-mailed me was, in fact, Frederick H. Boissevain, the son of Frederick W. Boissevain, the American who had been accidentally killed while observing a live ammunition training session at the Camp (see Chapter VII, "Deaths"). My asking questions regarding the current state of his father's health indicated to him that I had no idea of his father's fate and destroyed my credibility as a serious investigator.

As soon as I made the proper connection, I e-mailed back immediately with an apology and more detailed information. I received a reply simply asking, "Why was my father at Camp X?" We then continued our correspondence and shared the information which we each had.

* * *

In 1966, almost twenty years to the day after the closure of Camp X by the BSC, Walter McDayter, a staff reporter of the Toronto Telegram, ran into a Yugoslav who had been trained at Camp X and who had completed his mission in Yugoslavia. The agent informed McDayter about Camp X which was, of course, still top secret at that time. McDayter decided to investigate on his own. He went out and located Camp X. When he approached what he had been told was the Camp, he noted the country farm land, the old pitted dirt road leading to the Camp, and the numerous Department of National Defence signs that warned trespassers against getting any closer. The old original cow fence had been replaced by a larger, eight foot high barbed wire fence that surrounded the perimeter of the Camp, the same type of fencing that you would see surrounding a penitentiary today.

As he approached the fence in his vehicle, McDayter noticed a guard standing at the front gate with a pair of binoculars hanging around his neck. He also noticed that the guard was armed. Walter McDayter was warned to stay away, get back in his car and leave. But he had questions he wanted to ask.

Almost ten years later, I learned about Mr. McDayter's trip to the Camp. I contacted him and, when he answered the phone, I identified myself and told him that I, too, was investigating Camp X. His immediate reaction was, "Oh, that place! Those guys were crazy! They wanted to shoot me!"

McDayter had been told numerous times that if he persisted in taking pictures, he would be arrested. He continued in spite of the warning, so the armed guard came out and escorted him inside to a small room in one of the buildings where he was interrogated by officers and was told that, "This is a top secret military installation, no pictures are allowed to be taken, and no one is allowed in." He was sent on his way and told not to come back.

The interesting thing about the article he wrote relating the events of that day is that the Yugoslav agent that he had first encountered had told him that Igor Gouzenko had been under protection at Camp X shortly after the war had ended. Gouzenko was still alive and was being protected under a new name. It was big news at the time that Russian spies had been working in Canada. In retrospect, it now seems perfectly logical that they would have been, but at the time, most Canadians were unaware that Russian spies were walking amongst them.

The article talked about Gouzenko being kept at the Camp, and ended with the promise, "Tomorrow; Camp X and Igor Gouzenko". McDayter later told me that tomorrow never came for that next article.

He had been called into the General Manager's office at the Telegram and was informed that the second part of that article "would not run". Of course, when he asked why not, he was told it was a matter of military secrecy. The second part of the article never appeared!

The following series of photographs were taken in 1971, shortly before the Camp was destroyed and the property was prepared for the new Liquor Control Board of Ontario warehouse.

97. The original Guardhouse protecting the vacated Camp, 1971

98. The 'Glenrath Farm' road winds its way past the Communications Building which was a beehive of activity during World War II

99. The Commanding Officer's Quarters on the left was still in its original condition, and 'Hydra' on the right, unchanged but for the few scrapes and bruises that it suffered over the years, 1971

100. The eastern 'H' building (centre) which housed the Camp officers. To the far right, the agents' barracks, the only one of the original Camp X buildings that remains intact today, although it has been moved to another location

* * *

On a routine visit to Bob Stuart's Camp X Museum located in a temporary Quonset hut at the Oshawa Airport, I walked into the building and Bob was there, as usual, putting together displays of artifacts. I said to him, "Good morning, Bob."

Bob is a very secretive man of few words. He looked up at me and abruptly said, "Somebody was in here asking questions about you and what you were doing investigating into Camp X."

Considering all that I had been through to this point, inquiries such as this did not disturb me any longer. Later on, I found out that the "visitor" had been Nigel West, personally sent to Canada by Sir William Stephenson to investigate the backgrounds of those of us involved in the Camp X Museum Society. Even though I had spoken with Sir William many times by telephone, he was still, at this late stage of his life, the ever cautious "intelligence man" and still felt that it was his obligation to be on top of all political matters at all times.

* * *

On another occasion, I had been informed that there were a number of Camp X artifacts at Bayly Engineering in Ajax, only a few miles from Camp X. Benjamin de Forrest Bayly started Bayly Engineering immediately after the war and utilized much of the equipment that had been previously used at the Camp during the war. I followed the lead and pulled up in front of Bayly Engineering, parked my car and went in the front door. The receptionist asked me if she could help me and I said that I would like to speak with the manager. After a short period of time, a man of about fifty years of age came out to greet me.

Some pleasantries were exchanged, then I began to reveal exactly why I was there and what I hoped to see. I was abruptly told that it was none of my business, there was nothing to see and I was promptly escorted to the door and asked not to come back. I never did.

* * *

During the investigation, we would often arrange functions where ex-Camp X alumni could get together and talk about old times. These gatherings were tremendously successful and were talked about among the alumni community for some time afterwards.

One such function was the Camp X Reunion that was held in May of 1979 at the Oshawa Airport Museum and hosted by Robert Stuart, the curator. It was a marvelous night. People mingled about and the seemingly endless array of Camp X artifacts which were displayed on the tables right in front of us gave us a natural focus for conversation.

I remember one older gentleman whom I had never met before walked up to me and said, "Hi, how are you?"

I replied, "I'm fine, thank you."

He then said, "It's been a long time, hasn't it?"

"I'm sorry, I don't think that we've met."

The gentleman said, "You may not remember me, but I remember you very well. You used to come up from New York on a regular basis."

"You must be mistaken. I was never at the Camp."

He looked around very cautiously, then whispered, " It's O.K. We can talk about it now."

I did not want to embarrass the man by telling him that I was born just a few months after the Camp was closed down by the BSC, so I whispered back, "Well, one can never be too careful." From that point, using my extensive knowledge of the players involved in Camp X, we went on to have a delightful discussion about life at Camp X during the war years.

* * *

In 1979, my late father, George Hodgson, informed me that he and my mother would be vacationing that year in England. As he was now retired, Dad could take as much time as he liked and would have no problem in finding a place to stay given all his relatives who still lived there.

As one who was born in England and enjoys studying her history, my father would certainly be taking in many museums and sight-seeing spots. I asked him if he would do me a favour while he was there. Would he please look up a Mr. Boxshall of the Foreign and Commonwealth Office and deliver a parcel to him for me, saving me a lot of time writing back and forth to England. If you recall from earlier in the book, Mr. Boxshall was my contact for confirmation of data that I had obtained regarding Camp X.

I gave my father a list of questions for Mr. Boxshall, some photographs, and some documents that would indicate to him that I was a credible researcher. Dad put all of the things that I gave him into a plastic bag from a local supermarket and put them in his luggage. The next day my parents sailed for England. When they returned to Canada about twelve weeks later, Dad had a fantastic story to tell.

It started with a phone call to Mr. Boxshall. Dad asked for an appointment and he was told to come the next day at 10:00 a.m. Mr. Boxshall asked my father if he knew where to find him and he answered, " The Imperial War Museum, isn't it?"

Mr. Boxshall replied, "Yes, just check in with the lady at reception."

The next morning, Dad was there on time and checked in as requested. The receptionist said, "Just walk down the hall and to the right you will see a 'lift' on the right hand side. Press the button and go to the second floor."

Dad walked to the elevator and pressed the button. He heard a noise and could tell that it was the elevator coming down to the first floor. As the door opened, my father was thinking to himself, "How could anyone get into this elevator. It's so small!" He told me later that he hardly fit. The elevator went to the second floor, the gate opened and Dad stepped out into a huge room about half the size of a football field and with a ceiling perhaps thirty feet high.

As he looked around, he saw only a man seated behind a desk and two empty chairs in front of the desk, all situated in the middle of the room. The man gestured for my father to come over.

"Please sit down, Sir," said the man. As my father did so, the man behind the desk introduced himself as Mr. Boxshall. He told my dad that, although he had never met me personally, he knew me very well from our years of correspondence regarding Camp X.

He then said something to Dad that would he would remember for the rest of his life. Mr. Boxshall asked my father, "Do you know where you are, Sir?"

Dad replied, "Yes, of course. The Imperial War Museum."

Mr. Boxshall replied, "Yes, sir, you are technically correct. But this very room that you are in is also the original Bedlam." As my father looked around the room, he noticed the bare brick walls with the metal bars still imbedded in them. This was the Bedlam lunatic asylum where, in the year 1247, hundreds of insane people were confined and shackled in this one room. One can only imagine the chaos and the noise; hence the phrase, "It's Bedlam in there!"

After the initial shock of discovering where he was, Dad was able to settle down for an interesting chat with Mr. Boxshall who said, "I am going to send you to see another gentleman, a 'Mr. X', if you do not mind. Here is his address. He lives out in the country and you should arrive in time for tea this coming Saturday. Would that be alright?" My father said of course, that would be perfectly fine with him. He thanked Mr. Boxshall and, as he walked toward the "lift", he was still in awe as he looked around the huge room. Dad was one of few people to see Bedlam as it is not open to the public.

Dad arrived at the appointed time that Saturday. He drove up the lane way of the old country estate, so beautiful with its English country gardens and flower beds and the tall trees lining the driveway. He parked the car, walked up to the front door, and rang the chimes. A butler came to the door, escorted him into the den and asked if he could bring him something. Dad replied, "Yes, please, a cup of tea would be great." The butler said that he would return shortly with the tea and that the man of the house would be with Dad directly.

The butler brought the tea and Dad waited for about ten minutes more. A distinguished looking gentleman walked into the room and said, by way of introduction, "I am sorry that I can not tell you my name, but nonetheless I am pleased to make your acquaintance." My father, not being used to this "Cloak and Dagger" scenario, just went along with the flow.

The man said, "I understand that you have brought some things to show me."

"Yes, my son is investigating Camp X in Canada and wanted me to show you these items."

"Where are you staying, Mr. Hodgson?", the man asked.

"At the Savoy Hotel for a couple of nights, and then with some relatives of mine," my father replied.

"Did you know that many of our agents during the war stayed at the

Savoy while they were awaiting debriefing from their missions?," Mr. X asked.

"No, I didn't. I'm afraid I'm not up to speed on this entire subject, Sir," replied my father.

Dad pulled out the plastic grocery bag, opened it, and, one by one, began to show the gentleman the items that were in it. Mr. X studied them carefully and silently for some time, then he slowly raised his head. "Do you mean to tell me that you have been walking the streets of London with 'top secret' documents in a plastic shopping bag?"

Dad did not know what to say. He quickly determined that he could be staying a lot longer in England than anticipated if he could not explain himself. He pleaded ignorance, explaining that he was merely a courier and that the man would have to direct any questions to his son. The man told my father that, in his country, these things were considered 'top secret' and were deemed to be so for life. He could not and would not comment on the items. My father thanked him for his time, departed quickly, and returned to London.

Dad never did find out the man's identity, but he did have a vacation which he would never forget!

* * *

101. Each year on November 11, at exactly 11:00 a.m., the survivors of Camp X gather for a Remembrance Day Service

* * *

I would be remiss if I did not mention how much I miss visiting with Vilma and Eric Curwain on those long ago Saturday afternoons, and how Eric and I would play chess for hours talking on and on about World War II, his and Vilma's experiences and, of course, about Camp X.

As irony would often have it, when I first heard of Eric Curwain and began looking for him, I was absolutely amazed to find out that for years he had lived only one block away from where I worked in Etobicoke, a borough of Toronto, Ontario. If only I had known of him earlier, we could have enjoyed many more years together instead of the few short years that we had. Eric was close to eighty when I met him back in the late seventies.

However, I do like to think that I filled some void in Eric's life as he suffered terribly for years with crippling arthritis and was in failing health for some time. I believe he truly enjoyed my companionship and welcomed the diversion.

* * *

In the earlier chapters, I talked about the role of the other important peripheral links which played such a significant role in the success of Camp X. The Oshawa Airport, during World War II, was a 'Commonwealth Air Training Base' for the RAF and RCAF where pilots would be trained to fly all types of aircraft.

In many ways, the proximity of the airport was also very convenient for the Camp X personnel. If, for example, a Camp X instructor needed a Tiger Moth airplane for training a new group of agents, he would simply get on the telephone to Oshawa and, after pulling some strings, the airplane would show up at Camp right on schedule, landing in the field adjacent to Corbett Creek.

It was also convenient for bringing in visiting dignitaries. Aircraft would arrive in the dead of night, a car would pull up on the tarmac, a figure would descend from the aircraft and into the awaiting car, all with precision timing. Within fifteen minutes, the visitor could be inside Camp X. Customs agents would not be a necessity in this instance as background checks had been completed days before by the RCMP in co-operation with the FBI.

Just as Camp X had its problems and misfortunes, so did the Oshawa Training School. The following pictures show an aircraft in trouble as it tried desperately to land. Its entire training crew was lost in the tragedy.

102. The plane flies in low over the Tower. People can be seen running in different directions while those on the Tower balcony can only look up, frozen in horror and disbelief.

103. The plane clips the back part of the Tower building and veers straight up, breaking off the left wing. A man stands helplessly by

104. All that remains are the charred remnants of the plane and her crew

105. Bernie Sandbrook and Bill Hardcastle, Judi Longfield (back), Marlene Hodgson (front), Alan Longfield (back), Michael Longfield (front), and Renee Hodgson at the Camp X Memorial Wall dedication, 1984

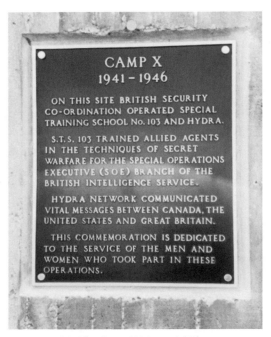

106. The Camp X Memorial Plaque

107. Sir William and Mary Stephenson

Inside-Camp X

Closing

*W*hy was Camp X opened?
Camp X was opened where it was because the surrounding area was rich in its ethnic makeup, facilitating the recruitment of agents from each of the national backgrounds required. There was an urgency in recruiting these agents as World War II was well into its second full year by the time that Camp X was opened.

The significance of Camp X has been undermined by some worldly scholars in that it was considered a 'PRIMARY' school of the SOE, and thus was thought to have little if any contribution to the outcome of World War II. In fact, it was a finely tuned machine turning highly qualified recruits into fully trained secret service agents of all ethnic backgrounds, readied and made available to the SOE on a moments notice. Even at this early stage of the war, the SOE simply had to send out the word, a "take-out order" if you will, to, "Please send eight well trained Yugoslav agents by September end, 1942." Weeks before the required date, eight well-trained agents were sailing to Britain, ready and eager for their assignments. The same would apply were the required agents French Canadians, Italians, Hungarians, Rumanians, Chinese or Japanese.

Many other peripheral functions conducted at Camp X were of great value to the war effort:

· The perfection of RDX explosives and the imagination required to best utilize this new-found wonder.
· The forged documents division of 'Station M' (BSC).
· The 'Secret Inks' training.
· The creation of 'Hydra', the most secret, sophisticated and important transmitting link between Britain and the United States.
· The creation by the Camp X instructors of the American counterparts, COI, OSS and CIA.

* * *

I would be remiss if I did not mention the controversy over the Reinhard Heydrich assassination in Czechoslovakia. Heydrich, "The Butcher of Prague," was, of course, the head of the Nazi's SD (Sicherheistsdienst), the intelligence and counter-espionage arm of the SS.

It has been written elsewhere that the Heydrich assassination conspiracy was hatched and planned at Camp X. As intriguing as this sounds, I must dispel the myth.

We know the following to be facts;

1. There were no Czechoslovakian agents trained at Camp X.

2. The first agents did not arrive until late January, 1942 and they were Americans working for the OSS.

3. The buildings were not completed until late January, 1942. In fact, the CO had to stay in the Sinclair farmhouse until his quarters were finished.

4. Heydrich was assassinated on May 27, 1942.

5. The CO and some of the Instructional Staff arrived at Camp X on December 6, 1941. Most of the balance of the Staff did not arrive until May and June of 1942.

6. It is inconceivable that the SOE would send an assassination team to Canada, to a Camp that was not even built yet and where there were no instructional staff to train for a mission which turned out to be one of the most important in all of World War II!

7. I have in my possession a taped interview with the very first Camp guard who was posted to the Camp on December 6, 1941, and relieved the night watchman from his duty of guarding the buildings still under construction at that time.

8. Finally, the assassination was carried out by two MI-6 agents named Jan Kubis and Josef Gabcik under the code name "Anthropoids." They parachuted into Bohemia in December of 1941 with three other agents and quickly met up with the resistance in a town called Lidice. There they remained in hiding for six months until they were able to assassinate Heydrich on May 27, 1942, in Prague.

It is also important to point out the terrible price that the town of Lidice paid for its role in the assassination of Reinhard Heydrich. Adolf Hitler was so incensed that the people of Lidice would collaborate with the agents that he put forward an edict calling for all of the men from the town of Lidice to be summarily lined up and shot. Its women and children were sent off to concentration camps, and the town was razed to the ground. When the Nazis finished with Lidice, one would not know that the town ever existed.

* * *

Recently released SOE files out of London, England, tell of an assassination plan that makes the Heydrich assassination appear insignificant. The plan took place in late 1944 and 1945, well after the SOE had left Camp X. The target was in 'X' Section, Germany, the plan was known as 'Operation Foxley', and the objective was Adolf Hitler himself!

The assassination plan was very similar to the successful Heydrich assassination and was in the practice stage when word came that Hitler had committed suicide on April 30, 1945. There was also a second assassination plan for 'X' Section, called 'Little Foxley.' The target this time was Dr. Joseph Goebbels, the German Propaganda Minister. This also was in the training stage when the Russians discovered his remains in 1945.

* * *

Many years later, Eric Curwain would write about Bill Stephenson, "*Had the British Secret Service during the postwar period been headed by a man of the calibre of a William Stephenson, it would never have given the impression of a football team directed by a myopic coach. However brilliant the undisclosed exploits of its individual operators may have been since the war, the Service's overall performance has been effectively neutralized by war, the Service's overall performance has been effectively neutralized by the information its defectors have divulged to Russia, at the same time bringing death to an unknown number of British agents behind the Iron Curtain."*

Eric had a great sense of humor as can be attested to by a quote from *Almost Top Secret,* "*Meanwhile over Norway, the Germans were on the march northwest, while the Allied ships and planes did their best to halt them. A Canadian who later joined our SIS unit was a radio operator on an American merchant ship at the time of the German invasion of Norway.*

"*His vessel happened to be docked at Trondheim when a British Coastal Command plane badly damaged the cruiser Konigsberg there. Murray, the Canadian operator, was watching from a hotel balcony standing beside some German officers who shouted with joy when they saw a British plane drop like a falling leaf above the cruiser. 'He's been shot down!,' they cried out. The plane continued its dive and dropped a bomb down the ship's funnel.*"

* * *

Early on in the investigation of Camp X, I often asked the people involved, "Why all the secrecy after all these years?" It is only recently that I have begun to understand why people involved in the intelligence departments did not want to talk about their missions or their involvement in the war.

In answer to one of my questions regarding some of the Camp X staff, E. G. Boxshall of the Foreign and Commonwealth Office wrote, "As ex-members of SOE signed the Official Secrets Act, they are not permitted to disclose any details about their war-time service in the SOE or BSC organizations."

Throughout Europe as the war ended, people quickly took to the streets pointing fingers at their neighbours, identifying them as Nazi collaborators. People were hanged in the streets as traitors, without benefit of a trial. Of these, many were not only innocent but were, in fact, actually heroes. It must be remembered that all the agents had phony aliases. Given the covert operations of agents and double agents, the average person on the street could easily jump to incorrect conclusions about any given individual's activities.

The following actual situation best sums up why a secret agent would want to keep his or her mission quiet and take it to the grave. Levon Aghazarian, an Armenian, whose brother, Flight Lieutenant Jack Aghazarian's, name is the first one listed on the SOE monument at Valencay, France, has posted a standing offer of a reward in the amount of ten thousand pounds for information identifying the informant who exposed his brother to the Gestapo.

* * *

And what became of the 'Start Up' Camp X Personnel?

Lieutenant-Colonel Arthur Terence Roper-Caldbeck, after returning to England, awaited his next assignment. On November 13, 1943, he was posted to the Central Mediterranean Forces as Commander of another SOE training school.

On November 22, 1944, he left CMF and was re-posted to the U.K. On February 19, 1945, he was 'out-posted' from SOE to 8 Infantry Holding Battalion.

No further records are available but we do know that he lived to see a normal retirement.

* * *

Lieutenant-Colonel Richard Melville (Bill) Brooker, in May of 1942, was loaned for three months to the OSS to assist in starting training schools in the USA (such as RTU-11 in Maryland).

In August of 1942, he was appointed Commandant of STS 103 and promoted to Lieutenant-Colonel. On April 5, 1943, he arrived in the UK from Montreal and was posted to Algiers for three months service with SOE in North Africa.

The OSS requested his permanent service for Canada and the USA, so Lieutenant-Colonel R.M. Brooker was transferred from the SOE to the OSS on June 1, 1944. No further information is recorded about his subsequent service with the OSS.

* * *

Lieutenant-Colonel Cuthbert Skilbeck, following the closure of STS 103, arrived back in the UK on April 28, 1944, and effective August 12, 1944, he was out-posted from the SOE to the Political Intelligence Department of the FO (Foreign Office) for 'special duties' Political Warfare Executive.

As did Roper-Caldbeck and Brooker, Skilbeck lived to see a ripe old age.

* * *

Lieutenant-Colonel William Ewart Fairbairn was lent to the OSS by the SOE in May of 1942 as a paramilitary instructor. At the request of the

OSS, Major Fairbairn was released by the SOE and transferred to Etousa on May 5, 1944 for service with the OSS in the USA until cessation of hostilities.

He was simultaneously granted promotion to Acting Lieutenant-Colonel on May 5, 1944, and he left the OSS in August of 1945.

Lieutenant-Colonel Fairbairn wrote the following books about his special training methods:

All in Fighting, published in 1942 by Faber & Faber Ltd.; *Get Tough;* and *Hands OFF,* published in the USA.

* * *

Major James (Paddy) Adams returned to the UK on August 7, 1942, and was appointed O.C. (Officer Commanding) W/T Station 53. On August 22, 1944, Adams was appointed O.C. Massingham W/T Station in North Africa.

On September 9, 1944, he was transferred to and appointed O.C. Middle East W/T Station. On November 2, 1944 Adams was transferred to 'Force 136' India Command. On July 13, 1945, James Adams ceased to be employed by the SOE. No further information is available.

* * *

Major Arthur Jackson Bushell remained as Camp 'Adjutant-Quartermaster' until January 5, 1944, when he was promoted to Major. Bushell would finish out the war years at Camp X.

* * *

Major Frederick Stanley Milner returned to the UK from Camp X on April 18, 1943, and was transferred to SOE in North Africa on May 12, 1943, for liaison work with the American forces.

On October 21, 1944, Milner returned from Africa and was transferred to SOE in New Delhi (Force 136). Major Milner did valuable work fighting the Japanese, for which he was awarded the 'Military Cross'. No further information is available.

* * *

Sergeant-Major George de Rewelyskow, at the end of his term at Camp X, returned to the SOE in Britain for reassignment. The SOE was so in need of good, experienced and talented agents that he was asked to go into the field on several dangerous missions. On one such mission, in Burma, Sergeant-Major George de Rewelyskow was killed in action.

* * *

Many other British instructors would go through Camp X but mostly for short periods of time. Little public information is available about these men.

108. This picture was taken in April of 1999 from Bill Hardcastle's house, not far from Camp X. Note to the far right the beach area and the thirty foot bluffs

How I long to walk just one more time along the laneway that weaves through Camp X. But that will never happen. In someone's misdirected wisdom, the magnificent historical significance of Camp X was deemed not very interesting and thus not worth preserving.

Lynn-Philip Hodgson

Inside - Camp X

The Letters

I have in my possession a number of letters that were written between Camp X personnel and Military District No. 2 in Toronto. I would like to share these with you as I believe that they will give you a more colourful insight into how the Camp was set up and operated.

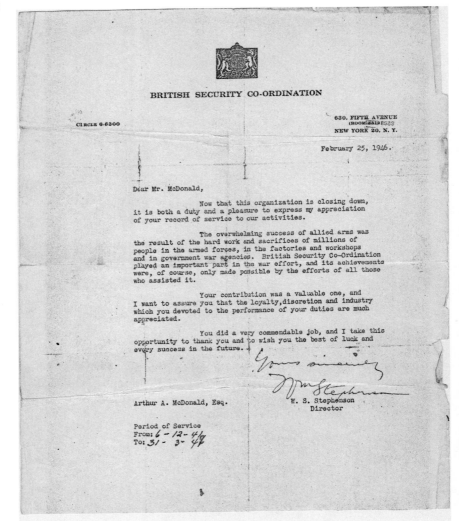

BRITISH SECURITY CO-ORDINATION

CIRCLE 6-6300

630, FIFTH AVENUE
(ROOM 3513 3553)
NEW YORK 20. N. Y.

February 25, 1946.

Dear Mr. McDonald,

Now that this organization is closing down,
it is both a duty and a pleasure to express my appreciation
of your record of service to our activities.

The overwhelming success of allied arms was
the result of the hard work and sacrifices of millions of
people in the armed forces, in the factories and workshops
and in government war agencies. British Security Co-Ordination
played an important part in the war effort, and its achievements
were, of course, only made possible by the efforts of all those
who assisted it.

Your contribution was a valuable one, and
I want to assure you that the loyalty, discretion and industry
which you devoted to the performance of your duties are much
appreciated.

You did a very commendable job, and I take this
opportunity to thank you and to wish you the best of luck and
every success in the future.

Yours sincerely,

W. S. Stephenson
Director

Arthur A. McDonald, Esq.

Period of Service
From: 6 - 12 - 44
To: 31 - 3 - 44

*The first letter is one received by Mac McDonald, one of the guards
at Camp X, from Sir William Stephenson.*

T.S 24-1

Headquarters, Military District No. 2,
159 Bay Street, Toronto, Ontario,

PERSONAL &
SECRET

CANCELLED

7th December, 1941.

Colonel W.H.S. Macklin, B.A.Sc.,
    Director of Staff Duties,
        Woods Building,
            Ottawa, Ontario.

        Col. Roper Coldbeck arrived yesterday and
is looking about. Adjutant, cooks, etc. proceed to-morrow
and they will get the place running. He seems very
pleased with arrangements so far.

2.   We have supplied stationery according to
the enclosed list. I am sending this to you so that you
can fix it with Stationery Branch in order that we get
re-embursed. They also need a duplicating machine and
paper, waxes, inks, etc., to use with it. Will you please
get Stationery to ship them at once to me personally for
"project J"? > without disclosing anything.

3.   In order to preserve secrecy, we have
named this affair "project J" and numbered it "special 25-1-1".
Pay, Ordnance, Medicals, Records, etc. must have something
although they don't know when or what it is. I keep all
our correspondence separate from the routine 25-1-1 (locked
in my desk). The attached memo shows the routine. Also
receipted voucher for stationery already issued.

        Yours sincerely,

        (C. F. Constantine)
        Major-General
        District Officer Commanding
        Military District No.2

copies of list given to Dagus.

Note the date confirming Roper-Caldbeck's arrival — December 7, 1941!

Special 25-1-1,
c/o Headquarters, Military District No.2.

Toronto, Ontario.
21st December, 1941.

Major-General C.F. Constantine, D.S.O.,
District Officer Commanding,
Military District No.2,
159 Bay Street,
Toronto, Ontario.

Dear General Constantine:-

It is impossible for me to thank you
sufficiently for the invaluable assistance you have
given me in the task of organizing Project "J".

Major Wilkes has been of tremendous help to
me, as have all the other Members of your Staff, with
whom I have come in contact. Not only have they
given me all the help they possibly could, but they
have asked no questions and have treated me like an
old friend when I am, in reality, a stranger. It is
my first visit to Canada and I have been overcome
with the friendliness and cooperation of your Staff.

Things are beginning to run fairly smoothly
at the Camp, and Lieut. Bushell and Sgt. Maloney are
doing excellent work and have been of great help to
me.

We have not yet gotten our complete Staff
together as certain men have not proved suitable,
but Lieut. Bushell is in close touch with District
Depot and suitable men will be available shortly.

There is one point that I would like to
raise regarding the local Press. As it is necessary
to use explosives of various types at this Camp, I
anticipate receiving enquiries from the Press regarding
the nature of the Training being carried out. If, and
when, these enquiries are received, I have issued
instructions to All Ranks under my Command that they
must be referred to the District Officer Commanding,
Military District No.2. If I may, I would like to
suggest that your Press Liaison Officer might explain
that we are experimenting with various types of
explosive, the nature of which it is not desirable
to be made public, and that a Defense "Stop" be put
on the Press.

As soon as we are properly settled in, and
are fully organized, I hope, very much indeed, that
you will be able to find time to visit the Camp.

Thank you again for your kind help and
cooperation.

Yours sincerely,

A.T.Roper-Caldbeck, Lieut-Col.,
Officer Commanding,
Special 25-1-1.

Lieutenant-Colonel Roper-Caldbeck sent a thank you letter to Major-General Constantine, District Commanding Officer, Military District #2, in which he suggested an ingenious plan to divert the local press in order to maintain the necessary secrecy regarding the true purpose of the Camp. He sought and received approval to invite the press to the Camp to convince them that the reason for the Camp's existence was solely for the purpose of testing new explosives badly needed for the war effort. From this point on, the Camp was known among the press as an explosives testing site and a Canadian Broadcasting Centre (CBC) station.

Special 25-1-1

Headquarters, Military District No. 2,
159 Bay Street, Toronto, Ontario,
23rd December,   1

Lieut.-Colonel A.T. Roper-Caldbeck,

Dear Colonel Caldbeck,

      I am so glad to know that the
arrangements are working out satisfactorily
to you except in the case of a few odd personnel.
The latter I fear one cannot be sure of this
side of the grave as there are the human frailties
and nature to contend with.

      With regard to your explosions and
the local press, I am seeing my Press Liaison
fellow within the next two minutes and shall instruct him to take adequate action.

      We are feeling a bit down here this
afternoon as we have just got word that Lawson,
Commanding Canadians in Hong Kong, and his Senior
Staff Officer, Pat Hennessy, have been killed.

      Drewbrook has kindly said he would let
me know when you were a going concern and that we
might go down together to call.

      All best wishes to you for Christmas
and New Year's,

          Yours sincerely,

          (C. F. Constantine)
           Major-General

Major-General Constantine addresses Roper-Caldbeck's concerns as expressed in his letter of December 21 regarding the local press, and informs Roper-Caldbeck of the death of two of their men in Hong Kong.

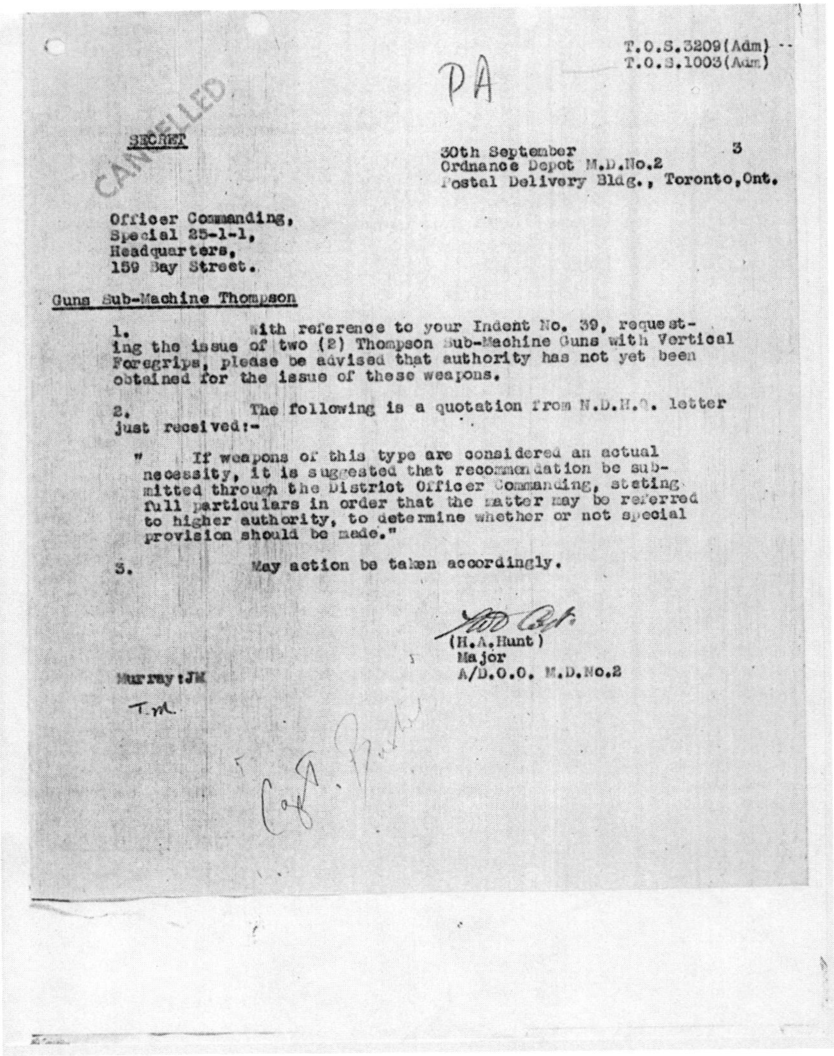

T.O.S.3209(Adm)
T.O.S.1003(Adm)

PA

SECRET

30th September
Ordnance Depot M.D.No.2
Postal Delivery Bldg., Toronto,Ont.

3

Officer Commanding,
Special 25-1-1,
Headquarters,
159 Bay Street.

Guns Sub-Machine Thompson

1.   With reference to your Indent No. 39, request-
ing the issue of two (2) Thompson Sub-Machine Guns with Vertical
Foregrips, please be advised that authority has not yet been
obtained for the issue of these weapons.

2.   The following is a quotation from N.D.H.Q. letter
just received:-

"   If weapons of this type are considered an actual
necessity, it is suggested that recommendation be sub-
mitted through the District Officer Commanding, stating
full particulars in order that the matter may be referred
to higher authority, to determine whether or not special
provision should be made."

3.   May action be taken accordingly.

(H.A.Hunt)
Major
A/D.O.O. M.D.No.2

Murray:JM

The request goes in for two Thompson Sub-Machine Guns.

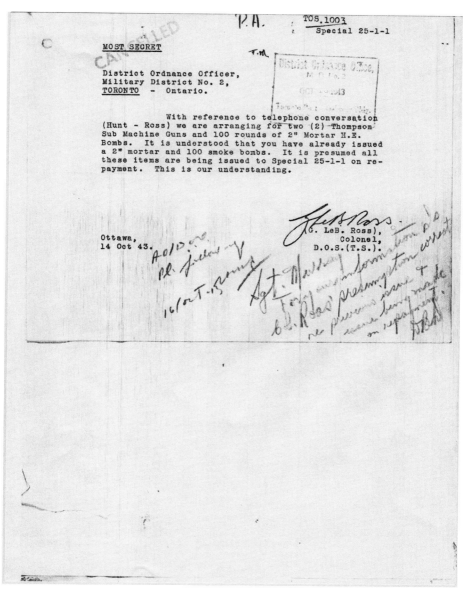

P.A.

TOS.1003

Special 25-1-1

MOST SECRET

District Ordnance Officer,
Military District No. 2,
TORONTO - Ontario.

        With reference to telephone conversation
(Hunt - Ross) we are arranging for two (2) Thompson
Sub Machine Guns and 100 rounds of 2" Mortar H.E.
Bombs. It is understood that you have already issued
a 2" mortar and 100 smoke bombs. It is presumed all
these items are being issued to Special 25-1-1 on re-
payment. This is our understanding.

Ottawa,
14 Oct 43.

G. LeB. Ross),
Colonel,
D.O.S.(T.S.).

Permission is granted for two Thompson Sub. Machine guns to be sent to STS-103

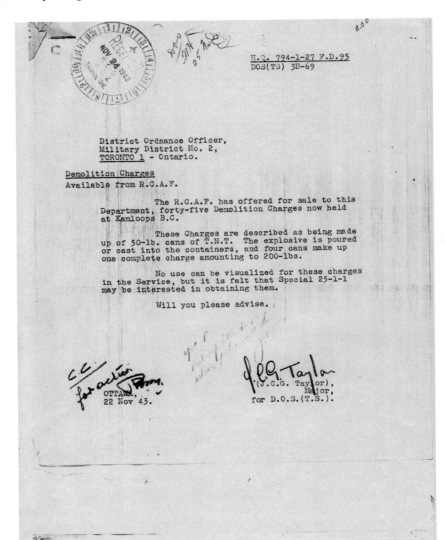

H.Q. 794-1-27 F.D.95
DOS(TS) 3B-69

District Ordnance Officer,
Military District No. 2,
TORONTO 1 - Ontario.

Demolition Charges
Available from R.C.A.F.

The R.C.A.F. has offered for sale to this
Department, forty-five Demolition Charges now held
at Kamloops B.C.

These Charges are described as being made
up of 50-lb. cans of T.N.T. The explosive is poured
or cast into the containers, and four cans make up
one complete charge amounting to 200-lbs.

No use can be visualized for these charges
in the Service, but it is felt that Special 25-1-1
may be interested in obtaining them.

Will you please advise.

(J.C.G. Taylor),
Major,
for D.O.S.(T.S.).

OTTAWA,
22 Nov 43.

There was nothing that Camp X would turn away

IN REPLY PLEASE QUOTE No. **9-1**   TOS.1003

DEPARTMENT OF NATIONAL DEFENCE

CANADA

A R M Y   Special 25-1-1,
c/o Headquarters, M.D. #2,
159 Bay St., Toronto, Ont.,
2nd December, 1943.

SECRET.

DEC 4 1943
Toronto Postal Delivery Bldg.
TORONTO, - ONT.

District Ordnance Officer,
Postal Delivery Building,
Toronto, Ontario.

Demolition Charges
Available from R.C.A.F.

Reference your TOS. 1003 dated 29th November, 1943, regarding the m/n subject.

2.   The explosives mentioned in this letter can be used by this organization and we shall be glad to receive them at your early convenience.

3.   May we be advised please regarding the approximate cost of these demolition charges if you are in possession of this information.

A. J. Bushell, Capt. & Adjt.,
for C. Skilbeck, Lieut-Colonel,
Officer Commanding,
Special 25-1-1.

C.C.
For action.

NAT. DEF. B. 440

DND finds a home for their explosives

M.F.D. 857	**DEPARTMENT OF NATIONAL DEFENCE**	Purchase Order

ROYAL CANADIAN ORDNANCE CORPS

OFFICE OF THE DISTRICT ORDNANCE OFFICER

No. 1533.....

(In any correspondence upon this subject please quote the above number.)

At Toronto, Ontario. .... Date 7th September, 1943.

To Department of Munition & Supply, 11 Jordan Street, Toronto, Ontario.

It is requested that you supply the following stores or service for this depot for which payment will be made in due course.

Stores to be DELIVERED to Ordnance Depot, Bay & Fleet Sts., Toronto, Ontario.

Invoices in QUINTUPLICATE to be MAILED to Ordnance Officer, Bay & Fleet Sts., Toronto.

Description of articles or service to be performed	No. or Quantity	Rate $ c.	Amount $ c.
			F.E. 0004
CARTRIDGES S.A.			
.32 Automatic Rds.	6000	22.00M	
.380 Colt Automatic Rds.	5000	37.00M	
			317 00
To be taken to charge			
Due out to Spec. 25-1-1			
Indent T.8233			
C Group – Q-1 section			

(Signed) J.H. Bell Capt. for A/Chief .... District Ordnance Officer, M.D. No. .....2.....

11,000 rounds of ammunition will keep the Camp X agents busy

lfr

Department of National Defence

Ottawa, Canada,

24 OCT 41

QUOTE No. H.Q.S.8885
(DSD)

MOST SECRET & PERSONAL

CANCELLED

CANADA

Dear General Constantine:-

1.   C.G.S. has asked me to write to you personally regarding the matter discussed below in order that it may be kept secret.

2.   The British Government is setting up a Special Training School at Whitby, Ontario. The accommodation is already being built there.

3.   The Commandant will be a Colonel Lindsay of the British Army and he will provide the instructional staff and the students (16 in number). He will run a series of courses.

4.   We have been asked to find certain assistance in the way of Administrative Staff and Transport, etc. Details are at Appendix "A".

5.   The British will pay for all the assistance they get from us.

6.   The Minister has approved all this and has also approved a proposition that we do not set this unit up as a distinct unit of the Canadian Army. This avoids approach to P.C.

7.   We have thought it advisable to have the staff selected from M.D. No.2. The method of finding the personnel, therefore, will be as follows:

   (a) You should select them carefully with a view to picking reliable men who can keep quiet about their duties.

   (b) As far as possible they should be category men if you have such available.

   (c) When they are selected they will be posted to No. 2 District Depot on whose strength they will be carried and they will then be attached for duty to the Special Training School.

8.   Accounts in connection with the expenses of this school will be kept separately, as they are recoverable from the British Government. We will inform you later as to how and to whom these accounts are to be rendered. Accounts should include all charges, of whatever sort, properly chargeable against the school including pay and allowances, rations for both staff and students, etc., etc.

Major-General C.F. Constantine, D.S.O.,
   Headquarters, Military District No.2,
      Toronto, Ontario.

4

/2.

Nat. Def. A-168

The Camp X announcement, October 24, 1941

- 2 -

9.   Equipment and transport will be issued by
Ordnance to the Special Training School and accounted
for in the normal way.

10.   It is essential that the staff be all selected
and ready for duty before 15 November.

11.   Col. Lindsay is now in England but will be
returning in due course to start his school. In the
meantime any communications or queries you may have in
respect of this project should be addressed to:-

            Mr. T.G. Drewbrook,
            1130 Bank of Commerce Building,
            Toronto.

            Office Telephone   WA 4561.
            House Telephone   RA 1394.

12.   I would suggest that you get in touch with
Mr. Drewbrook who will no doubt be glad to discuss the
matter with you in more detail than I am able to do in
this letter. The Minister's intention is that we give the
British every assistance in running this school, which is
regarded as an important one.

13.   C.G.S. asked me to impress the need for every
precaution as regards secrecy. The officer selected to be
Adj. and Q.M. should, therefore, be a very reliable type.
Perhaps you could arrange for some selected staff officer to
look over the men before they go on the job. They do not
need to know the purpose of the school as their work is purely
administrative.

14.   The file on this subject has had a very restricted
circulation here and therefore any correspondence on this
subject should be addressed:-

            Col. W.H.S. Macklin,
            Director of Staff Duties,
            Woods Building,
            Ottawa.

and should be marked "Most Secret and Personal".

15.   Please acknowledge receipt of this letter.

            (W.H.S. Macklin)
            Colonel,
            Director of Staff Duties.

3

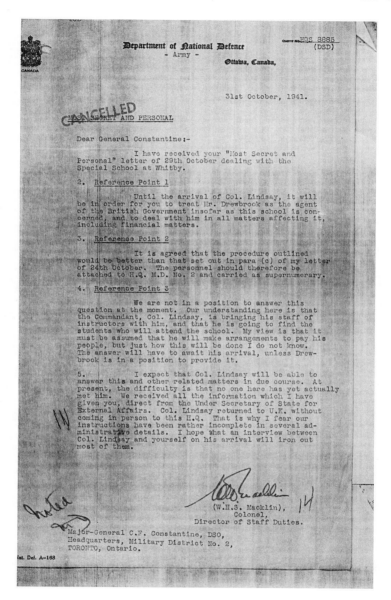

Department of National Defence
- Army -

Ottawa, Canada,

Quote No. HQS 8885
(DSD)

31st October, 1941.

~~CANCELLED~~

MOST SECRET AND PERSONAL

Dear General Constantine:-

I have received your "Most Secret and Personal" letter of 29th October dealing with the Special School at Whitby.

2. **Reference Point 1**

Until the arrival of Col. Lindsay, it will be in order for you to treat Mr. Drewbrook as the agent of the British Government insofar as this school is concerned, and to deal with him in all matters affecting it, including financial matters.

3. **Reference Point 2**

It is agreed that the procedure outlined would be better than that set out in para (c) of my letter of 24th October. The personnel should therefore be attached to H.Q. M.D. No. 2 and carried as supernumerary.

4. **Reference Point 3**

We are not in a position to answer this question at the moment. Our understanding here is that the Commandant, Col. Lindsay, is bringing his staff of instructors with him, and that he is going to find the students who will attend the school. My view is that it must be assumed that he will make arrangements to pay his people, but just how this will be done I do not know. The answer will have to await his arrival, unless Drewbrook is in a position to provide it.

5. I expect that Col. Lindsay will be able to answer this and other related matters in due course. At present, the difficulty is that no one here has yet actually met him. We received all the information which I have given you, direct from the Under Secretary of State for External Affairs. Col. Lindsay returned to U.K. without coming in person to this H.Q. That is why I fear our instructions have been rather incomplete in several administrative details. I hope that an interview between Col. Lindsay and yourself on his arrival will iron out most of them.

(W.H.S. Macklin),
Colonel,
Director of Staff Duties.

Major-General C.F. Constantine, DSO,
Headquarters, Military District No. 2,
TORONTO, Ontario.

lat. Del. A-168

Colonel Lindsay never returned to Canada, therefore the first Official Commandant of Camp X was, in fact, Lieutenant-Colonel Roper-Caldbeck

QUOTE No. H.Q.S. 8865 (D.S.D.)

Department of National Defence
- Army -

Ottawa, Canada.

CANADA

MOST SECRET AND PERSONAL   29th October, 1941.

Dear General Constantine:-

       I have received your "Most Secret and Personal" letter of 27th October dealing with the Special Training School at Whitby.

2.   I have discussed the matter of Medical Services with D.G.M.S., who says that he considers that Medical Services can be provided by the local D.P.N.H. physician, Dr. R.T. MacLaren of Whitby.

3.   He suggests your D.M.O. should make local arrangements with D.P.N.H. representative for such services. The D.M.S. of D.P.N.H. here is agreeable.

4.   I asked D.G.M.S. if a medical orderly is necessary on the Administrative Staff. He thinks not. Nevertheless, if the Commandant should want one, I think we should meet his requirement. As I said in a previous letter, the general policy is to help the British as much as necessary to get this school going and make it work.

      (W.H.S. Macklin)
      Colonel,
    Director of Staff Duties

Major-General C.F. Constantine, DSO,
Headquarters, Military District No. 2,
TORONTO, Ontario.

NAT. DEF. A-168-A
600M—3-40 (4472-3-4)
H.Q. 1772-30-376

The wheels of STS-103 are in motion

T/S 24-1

Headquarters, Military District No. 2,
159 Bay Street, Toronto, Ontario,
29th October, 41.

REGISTERED

MOST SECRET AND PERSONAL

Colonel W. H. S. Macklin, B.A.Sc.,
    Director of Staff Duties,
        Woods Building,
            Ottawa, Ontario.

Dear Macklin:

          I have been in touch with Mr. Drewbrook
and discussed the matters mentioned in your H.Q.S.
8885 (D.S.D.) of the 24th instant.

          Some minor points have arisen which I should
like cleared up. They are -

(1) Pending the arrival of Col. Lindsay from England,
     I should like definite authority, please, for
     dealing direct with Mr. Drewbrook in matters
     affecting finance, stores, etc., etc., unless
     you consider Para. 11 of your above quoted letter
     is sufficient authority.

(2) With regard to Para. 7(c) o your letter, for
     simplification of accounting and pay, as well as
     matters of secrecy, it is thought it would be
     better to attach the personnel to this District
     Headquarters, supernumerary for special duty,
     when all matters pertaining to pay, rations,
     clothing, etc., would be confined to a much smaller
     number of people. The Adjutant of the Detachment
     could issue local Part II Orders, supplying the
     necessary information for the compilation of pay
     sheets, ration accounts, etc., etc.

(3) How are the British personnel to be paid? through
     our pay accounts or direct by Drewbrook? The
     reason I bring this question up is that Col. Frenshaw
     and the other British officer attached to 5th
     Armoured Division, as well as Intelligence Officers
     at our Internment Camps, have had considerable dif-
     ficulties with regard to the obtaining of and the
     amount of pay due them.

          I see no difficulties in obtaining the personnel
required, or providing any of the equipment necessary.

          Mr. Drewbrook informs me that he has already
purchased mechanical transport, beds, bedding, crockery,
and various other articles, which will not, therefore, be
required from us, with the exception perhaps of some
supplementary transport.

          He also informs me that the date of the opening
of this school has now been set as 1st December and not
15th November.

                              Yours sincerely,

Tommy Drew-Brook appears

SPECIAL TRAINING SCHOOL

Administrative Staff

(i) Personnel

Detail	Officers	S/Sergeants & Sergeants	Corporals	Rank and File	Total
Lieutenant - for duty as adjutant and quartermaster	1				1
Company-quartermaster-sergeant		1			1
Provost Corporal			1		1
Clerks Group "C"				2	2
Cooks "C"				3	3
Butcher "C"				1	1
Mess Orderlies - Officers' Mess				3	3
Sergeants' Mess				1	1
Students' Mess				3	3
Drivers, I.C.				2	2
Sanitary Duties				1	1
Storemen				2	2
Provost				3	3
General Duty				3	3
Total all ranks excluding att'd.	1	1	1	24	27

(ii) Table of Weapons and Ammunition

Detail	Number	Ammunition - rounds		
		On man or with gun	Reserve	Total
Pistols .38 inch	12	12	6	216
Rifles .303 inch	16	25	600	1000

(iii) Transport

Car, light	1
Station Wagon	1
Truck, 8-cwt.	1
Wireless Sets, No. 19	6

(iv) Equipment

~~Wireless Sets~~

Hand Grenades   as required.

*HQ·S 8885
(DSO
27-10-41
2*

October 27, 1941 - The requisition goes out for the Camp X staff

Special 25 - 1 - 1
% Headquarters, Military District No.2
TORONTO   CANADA

PERSONAL & CONFIDENTIAL -

Major-General C. F. Constantine, D.S.O.,
District Officer Commanding,
Military District No. 2,
159 Bay Street,
TORONTO, Ont.

Dear General Constantine:-

      Major Brooker and I have been thinking over
and discussing at considerable length the question of
the information which should be given to the Press,
if and when they start asking questions.

      In my last letter to you I suggested that the
Press should be told that we were experimenting with
various types of explosives.

      I now feel that it might be easier to keep the
Press quiet if your Press Liason Officer could take them
into his confidence and tell them a slightly fuller
story about our activities, saying he knows they will
keep the information to themselves.

      If they are not told a story of some kind, I am
rather afraid that they will start guessing and their
speculations might appear in the Press in a form likely
to attract considerable attention.

      I attach a suggested "story" which could be told
to the Press if they do start getting too inquisitive.

      Thanking you again for your help and co-operation.

      Yours sincerely,

A. T. Roper-Caldbeck.
Lt Col.

c.c. to
Mr. T. G. Drew-Brook

- ; Press Story : - with Press Liason Officer

*The plan is developed further for the disguise of STS-103 to avoid speculation by
the press as to its true purpose*

T/S 24-1

Headquarters, Military District No. 2,
159 Bay Street, Toronto, Ontario,

8th January,   /42.

PERSONAL & SECRET

Lt.-Col. A. S. Roper-Caldbeck,
     Toronto, Ontario.

Dear Roper-Caldbeck:

I have your undated letter regarding the question of the "story".

I have had a talk with my Press Liaison Officer on the subject. Incidentally, I have not told him of your special activities, but informed him that they were of such a nature that even I did not know exactly what you were doing and it was imperative that the press did not "speculate in print". He agrees with me on your suggestion that the best thing to do would be to have no gratuitous comment in the press, but, if the press were pestered by people wanting to know about happenings in your vicinity, they have a story to give them.

On that understanding I have given him the "story" as set out by you for confidential information of the press, but not to be used unless necessity arises.

I trust this will be satisfactory. I do feel that it is a solution and will probably stop any local chat which is likely to occur, as quickly as any other means.

Yours very truly,

(C. F. Constantine)
Major-General
District Officer Commanding
Military District No. 2

"The story" is finalized

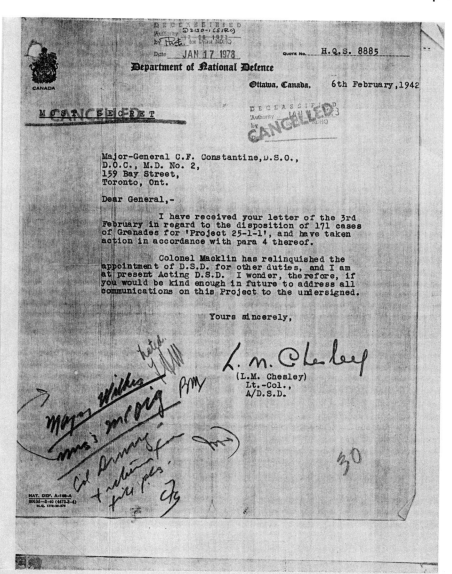

Quote No. H.Q.S. 8885

Department of National Defence

CANADA

Ottawa, Canada.   6th February, 1942

M.C.S. SECRET   CANCELLED

Major-General C.F. Constantine, D.S.O.,
D.O.C., M.D. No. 2,
159 Bay Street,
Toronto, Ont.

Dear General,-

I have received your letter of the 3rd
February in regard to the disposition of 171 cases
of Grenades for 'Project 25-1-1', and have taken
action in accordance with para 4 thereof.

Colonel Macklin has relinquished the
appointment of D.S.D. for other duties, and I am
at present Acting D.S.D. I wonder, therefore, if
you would be kind enough in future to address all
communications on this Project to the undersigned.

Yours sincerely,

(L.M. Chesley)
Lt.-Col.,
A/D.S.D.

More ammunition for the Camp; 171 cases of grenades

O.M.E. M.T. OFFICERS, 90 DAY INSPECTION SUMMARY—

This form has been prepared for the purpose of consolidating information from O.M.E. M.T. Officers' 90 Day Inspection Report Forms M.F.M. 261 - 262 - 263 covering inspection of Unit M.T. Maintenance and procedure and will be made in triplicate by the O.M.E. M.T. Inspecting Officer immediately upon completion of the above mentioned forms. Original will be mailed to the D. of M.M., N.D.H.Q., one copy to the D.O.C. and one copy retained by the O.M.E. M.T. Inspecting Officer for reference purposes. Since this is the only return reaching N.D.H.Q. in connection with Unit M. T. Maintenance in the field it is imperative that all information be accurate.

REMARKS:

Due to the nature of this Unit it is NOT permitted to visit or Inspect their Location.

Arrangements were made for their six (6) vehicles to report to Ordnance Workshop one at a time. The 90 Day and 5000 Mile Inspections were done and correction made as necessary. The vehicles were all passed back to the Unit Class "A".

This is the first time that ALL vehicles on their charge have passed through for 90 Day Inspection.

Log Books were checked for correct entires and the M.T. Clerk reported for instructions on GPM3 records. Their records were in accordance with instructions with small exceptions which are being corrected.

The motorcycle has been withdrawn from this Unit.

The Canadian Army is refused permission to inspect their own vehicles at Camp X

				Date recommendation passed forward	
				Received	Passed

.... Brigade .... Division .... Corps

Schedule No. .... Unit ...General List...
(to be left blank)

Army No. and Rank ...Captain...

Name ...Joseph Henri Adelard Benoit...
(Christian names must be stated)

Action for which commended (Date and place of action must be stated)	Recommended by	Honour or Reward	(To be left blank)
This officer was parachuted into France on ~~date~~ 23 May 44 to assist in building up a new circuit in the Reims area.

Time was too short for a great deal to be achieved but efficient small groups were built up at Reims and at Epernay. Benoit was chiefly responsible for the organization of the former group which he led in several sabotage operations on railways and telephone lines. He also armed 250 F.T.P. troops with arms captured from the Germans, and led them in mopping-up expeditions.

The results achieved by the Reims sabotage group were entirely due to Benoit's indefatigable energy and leadership, and his perseverance in the face of difficulties of every kind. It is recommended that he be appointed a Member of the Order of the British Empire.(Mil). | (sgd) C McV Gubbins

(sgd) HM Gale Lieutenant General Chief Administrative Officer | MBE | |

PTO

(BENOIT)

(Sir) Colin Gubbins, head of the SOE, commends the actions of Captain Joseph Henri Adelard Benoit, a Camp X trained agent

O R D E R No. 34

On proposal of the Minister for War

THE PRESIDENT OF THE PROVISIONAL GOVERNMENT OF THE REPUBLIC

MINISTER OF NATIONAL DEFENCE

MENTIONS IN A GENERAL ORDER TO THE ARMY

Captain Lionel Guy d'ARTOIS, dit Michel
of the Canadian Army.

"Canadian Officer, parachuted in Occupied
France (Saone et Loire) one month before the allied
invasion. Placed at the disposal of the Interior
French Forces his fine qualities of intelligence,
energy and character.
Organized and armed several important units
with which he participated with exceptional initiative
in numerous operations".

This mention carries the award of the "Croix de
Guerre avec Palme" and annuls order No. III of 5.9.44
of the Interior French Forces (Departement de Saone
et Loire).

General (Armee) JUIN   PARIS, this

(Sgd.) A. JUIN

(Sgd.) F. GOUIN

(d'Artois)

*Captain Lionel Guy d'Artois, another Camp X alumni, received the "Croix de
Guerre Avec Palme" from the government of France*

Index — Major Players

Photograph Credits

Photo #		Credit
1	*Front Cover*	Town of Whitby Archives, Mr. Brian Winter
2	*Intro by Andy Durovecz*	Author
3	*Intro by Lynn Hodgson*	Author
4	*Intro by Lynn Hodgson*	Author
5	*Chapter I*	Harry Smith
6		Harry Smith
7		Harry Smith
8		Harry Smith
9		Robert Stuart
10		Harry Smith
11		Harry Smith
12		Harry Smith
13		Harry Smith
14		Mac McDonald
15		Bill Hardcastle
16		Eric Curwain
17		Robert Stuart
18		Harry Smith
19	*Chapter II*	City of Oshawa
20		Robert Stuart
21		Town of Whitby Archives, Mr. Brian Winter
22		Town of Whitby Archives, Mr. Brian Winter
23		Harry Smith
24		Harry Smith

25		Harry Smith
26		Harry Smith
27		Harry Smith
28		Mac McDonald
29		Harry Smith
30		Harry Smith
31		Robert Stuart
32		Robert Stuart
33		Harry Smith
34		Harry Smith
35		Harry Smith
36		Robert Stuart
37		Harry Smith
38		Harry Smith
39		Bill Hardcastle
40		Ajax Community Archives
41		Ajax Community Archives
42		Ajax Community Archives
43		Ajax Community Archives
44	*Chapter III*	Robert Stuart
45		Robert Stuart
46		Author
47		Robert Stuart
48		Robert Stuart
49	*Chapter IV*	Eric Curwain
50		Author
51		Author
52		Author
53	*Chapter V*	Harry Smith
54		Harry Smith
55		Robert Stuart
56		Robert Stuart
57		Harry Smith
58		Harry Smith
59	*Chapter VI*	Courtesy of Ian D. Foster, Handley-Page 57 (Halifax) 'Rescue'
60		Andy Durovecz
61		Andy Durovecz
62		Andy Durovecz
63		Captain Peter Mason
64		Andy Durovecz
65		Robert Stuart
66		Andy Durovecz
67		Camp X Museum Society
68		Andy Durovecz
69		Courtesy of Ian D. Foster, Handley-Page 57 (Halifax) 'Rescue'
70		Robert Stuart
71		Robert Stuart
72		Harry Smith

Lynn-Philip Hodgson

References

Page Number

Introduction by Andy Durovecz

xiii-xiv   Quote by Sir Winston Churchill.

Introduction by Lynn-Philip Hodgson

xxi   Quote from Eric Curwain's unpublished manuscript, *"Almost Top Secret."*

Chapter I

3 - 8   The Introduction of the Camp X personnel - courtesy of E.G. Boxshall, Foreign and Commonwealth Office, London, England.

3   Quote by General (Sir) Colin Gubbins.

4   Quote from Bickham Sweet-Escott.

9 - 16   Quotes and interviews with Bill Hardcastle.

9 - 16   Quotes from (25-1-1, The Camp X Journal, Alan Longfield Editor)

160 - 166   Quotes by Walter McDayter, staff reporter for the Toronto Telegram.

162   Quotes by Robert Stuart, Camp X Museum.

Intelligence Departments

Abbreviations

OWI	—	Office of War Information
STS	—	Special Training School
SOE	—	Special Operations Executive
BSC	—	British Security Co-ordination
FBI	—	Federal Bureau of Investigation
SIS	—	Secret Intelligence Service
OSS	—	Office of Strategic Services
COI	—	Co-ordinator of Information

Inside - Camp X cuts through the mystery and intrigue and takes us on a fascinating journey behind the sentries and barbed wire and into the hearts and minds of ordinary men and women who, like so many at this critical point in history, answered the call to serve their country in time of need.

Half a century later, the ranks of those remaining seriously diminished, the window through which we peer into history will soon be closed effectively severing the link between those who lived history and those of us who only study it.

Recognizing the historical significance of the Camp, the Camp X Society, a not-for-profit organization, was established in 1998. The Camp X Society is dedicated to preserving the memory of those courageous men and women who were trained in subversive warfare and covert actions, those who lived in the shadows and served at the Camp.

The Camp X Society is dependent upon public subscription, donations and grants to carry out its work of researching and documenting the Camp's history, conserving Camp X artifacts and raising enough capital with which to fund a modest museum initiative. A portion of the proceeds from this book have been earmarked for the Camp X Society.

Thank You for your Support

Norm Killian
Director
Camp X Society 1999

(Author's Note: In fact, ten percent of the profits from Inside-Camp X will be donated to the Camp X Society)

Lynn-Philip Hodgson

INSIDE-CAMP X

The following poem was written by my old friend Eric Curwain (a.k.a. Bill Simpson), June 6, 1979, 35 years to the day after 'D' Day. Eric was the brains behind the recruitment of most of the staff and agents who would be trained at Camp X and go on to their most dangerous missions behind enemy lines.

Shortly before his death, Eric asked me to put his poem to good use. I can not think of a better place than in my book where Eric plays such a prominent role.

Canada on 'D' Day

The older sons of Canada
look down on Juno Beach:
They see the grieving men in prayer
and read the heart of each.

On Juno Beach they see the men
who landed at their side,
but were not called upon to sink
in sand or sullen tide.

And to the east there stands the stone
that marks the Vimy field,
where men had fought a thousand days
and never thought to yield.

Those Vimy heroes see their sons
in Normandy today
and all three bands - pere, fils et frere -
have common cause to pray.

For they can sense a mood of change,
of purpose unfulfilled:
they wonder if the future holds
what they had fought to build.

The men and wives from many lands

did weave our Tapestry -
let none contrive to make of it
a faded travesty.

O Canada! O Canada!
Thy patriot sons are we,
enfants de la Patrie.

Eric Curwain (a.k.a. Bill Simpson)

Québec, Canada
1999